DEEP

LEARNING

WITH PYTHON

*Comprehensive Guide of
Tips and Tricks using Deep Learning
with Python Theories*

ETHAN WILLIAMS

TABLE OF CONTENTS

Introduction

This book is designed to help you use Python for deep learning, including how to build and run deep learning models using Keras. This book also includes deep learning techniques, sample code, and technical content.

The mathematical foundations of deep learning are subtle: but the average user doesn't need to fully understand the mathematical details to pick up the keyboard and start programming. Practically speaking, deep learning is not complicated, but the results are very objective. Teach you how to use deep learning: this is the purpose of this book.

Deep Learning: How to Get Started Wrong!

If you ask the big guys how to get started with deep learning, what will they say? Nothing more than:

- Linear algebra is the key!

- You have to understand traditional neural networks to do it!

- Probability and statistics are the foundation, aren't they?

- You have to plunge in the water of machine learning for a few years before coming back.

- Don't talk to me if it's not a doctor of the computer!

- Getting started is simple: 10 years of experience should be almost enough. It's probably enough

- To sum it up: Only great gods can do deep learning.

Net TM nonsense!

1

Deep Learning with Python

This book is going to reverse the traditional teaching method: directly teach you how to deep learning. If you think this thing is really good, I need to study it carefully and then go into the technical details. This book directly lets you write what you can run with deep learning.

I use a lot of deep learning libraries: I think the best is Python-based Keras. Python is a complete and mature language that can be used directly at the core of commercial projects. R is not comparable to this. Compared with Java, Python has professional-level packages such as SciPy and Scikit-learn, which can quickly build a platform.

There are many deep learning libraries for Python, the most famous being Theano (dead, burnt paper) at the University of Montreal and Google's TensorFlow. Both libraries are simple, and Keras supports them seamlessly. Keras encapsulates the part of numerical calculations, leaving behind the key APIs for building neural networks and deep learning models.

This book will guide you to build neural networks and deep learning models yourself, and show you how to use them in your own projects. Stop talking nonsense and start quickly:

Book Structure

This book is divided into seven chapters:

- Course: Introduce a function of a neural network and how to write it using Keras API

- Project: Put the knowledge from the lesson together and write a project: This project can be used as a template

- Example: You can directly copy and paste the code! This book also comes with a lot of code that is freely available on Github!

Lessons and Projects

Each lesson is independent and is recommended to be completed at one time, with a duration of 20 minutes and several hours if you want to adjust the parameters carefully. The course is divided into four blocks:

- Background

- Multilayer perceptron

- Advanced Multilayer Perceptron and Keras

- Convolutional neural network

- And much more ...

Background

In this part, we introduce the three libraries Theano, TensorFlow (TF), and Keras, and how to test your network at low prices on Amazon Cloud Services (AWS). Divided into four parts:

- Getting started with Theano

- Getting started with TensorFlow

- Keras Getting Started

These are the most important deep learning libraries. Let's introduce a few more things:

- Project: Deploy a GPU project on the cloud

At this point, you should be ready to develop models with Keras.

Multilayer Perceptron

In this part, we introduce feed-forward neural networks and how to write your network with Keras. Roughly segmented:

- Getting started with multilayer perceptron

- Developing the first neural network with Keras

- Testing neural network model performance

- Machine learning with Scikit-Learn and Keras models

Three projects can help you create neural networks and layout templates for future networks:

- Project: Multi-Class Classification

- Project: Classification issues

- Project: Regression

At this point, you are familiar with the basic operations of Keras.

Advanced Multilayer Perceptron

In this part, we further explore Keras' API and study how to get the world's top results; content includes:

- How to save a neural network

- How to save the best network

- How to observe training results while training

- How to deal with overfitting

- How to improve training speed

At this point, you can already develop mature models using Keras.

Convolutional Neural Networks (CNN)

In this part, we introduce some computer vision and natural language problems and how to build a neural network with Keras to solve the problem well. The content includes:

- Introduction to Convolutional Neural Networks

- How to enhance the model effect

Write the code to understand the network: Here, we use CNN to solve the following problems:

- Project: Handwritten Character Recognition

- Project: Image Object Recognition

- Project: Film and Television Review Category

At this point, you can use CNN to deal with the actual problems you encounter.

Conclusion
In this part, we provide you with some information for further study.

Example

Accumulate code base as you learn: You write code for each problem for later use.

This book gives you code for all projects and some Keras code that is not covered. Build it yourself!

Book Requirements

Python and SciPy

You need at least Python and SciPy installed. By default, in this book, you have configured it. You can configure the environment on your machine, or in a virtual machine /Docker/cloud. See Chapter 2, Projects.

Software and libraries used in this book:

- Python 2 or 3: This book uses version 2.7.11.

- SciPy and NumPy: This book uses SciPy 0.17.0 and NumPy 1.11.0.

- Matplotlib: Version 1.5.1 for this book

- Pandas: This book uses version 0.18.0

- Scikit-learn: This book uses version 0.17.1.

The versions do not need to be precisely the same: but you don't want to install a version lower than the above requirements. The second part will walk you through configuring the environment.

Machine Learning

You don't need a professional background, but it will be helpful to study simple machine learning with Scikit-learn. Learn about basic concepts such as cross-checking. There are references at the back of the book: read them briefly.

Deep Learning

You don't need to know the mathematical theory of the algorithm, but the concepts need to be understood. This book has an introduction to neural networks and models but will not delve into the details. There are reference materials after surgery: I hope you have a little concept of neural networks.

Note: All examples can be run with the CPU. The GPU is not required, but the GPU can significantly speed up operations. Chapter 5 will show you how to configure the GPU on the cloud.

Book Objectives

I hope you have the ability to develop deep learning algorithms in Python from datasets after reading this book. Include:

- How to develop and test deep learning models

- How to use advanced tricks

- How to build large models for picture and text data

- How to expand image data

- How to ask for help

You can start now. You can read the topics you need, or you can go through the process from beginning to end. I recommend the latter.

I hope you make each example by yourself and record what you think. My email is jason@MachineLearningMastery.com. This book hopes you work hard and become a deep learning engineer as soon as possible.

What This Book Is Not

This book provides developers with an introductory tutorial on deep learning, but it has missed all. This book is not:

- Deep learning textbook: This book does not go into the technical details of neural networks, so please learn by yourself.

- Algorithm book: We don't pay attention to how the algorithm works; please learn by yourself.

- Python Programming Book: This book does not explain the use of Python in-depth; I hope you already know Python.

If you need to learn more about a topic, read the help behind the book.

Summary

At this moment, the tools of deep learning are at the peak of history, and the development of neural networks and deep learning has never been so fast, and it is amazing in countless fields, and we hope you have fun.

Chapter One

DEEP LEARNING METHODS AND APPLICATION

In the 2000s, artificial intelligence-based methods, which had been severely disrupted in the 2000s thanks to their deep learning approaches in the fields of natural language processing and machine learning, came to the fore again.

Although the number of hidden layers and nodes in artificial neural networks were increased, artificial intelligence methods were no longer used in the early 2000s due to insufficient hardware developments. However, as the costs of calculating artificial neural networks consisting of a large number of hidden layers have been reduced due to GPU and other hardware improvements, it has been re-used.

The deep learning approach consists of multiple processing layers combined with multiple abstraction structures to learn representations of data. The quality of machine learning approaches depends on the selection of the right features. To find these qualities, preprocessing, dimension reduction, and feature selection are performed. It is necessary to get rid of this dependence on features. Classifiers and other prediction

When designing systems, it may be easier to extract useful information from data with artificial intelligence. In this context, the issue of deep learning is closely related to representative learning. Deep learning algorithms have been applied to many different fields, especially after 2005. These studies will be explained in detail in this chapter.

Artificial Neural Networks

Artificial neural networks are modeled based on the learning techniques of the human brain. Therefore, firstly, biological nerve cells should be mentioned. If we examine the cell, the part that transmits signals from the cells to the nucleus is called dendrite. The structure that collects incoming signals is called (soma), and the structure that distributes this information to other cells is called the axon (axon).

The information from the axons is pre-treated with synaptic (synaptic) and transmitted to the dendrites of other cells. At this stage, signals are transmitted using threshold functions. The theory that learning takes place in synapses is still valid today.

Elements passing from biological nerves to artificial neural networks, neuron-processing, dendritic-aggregation function, cell body-activation function, axon-output, the synapse-weight conversion will transform.

Artificial neural networks are a system modeled based on the learning techniques of the human brain. First, in 1943, McCulloch and Pitts came up with a computational model, based on algorithms and math, for neural networks and called it threshold logic. This model has developed an approach that focuses on biological processes in the brain and the application of artificial intelligence neural networks.

Later in the same decade, Donald Hebb, a psychologist, based a learning hypothesis on Hebbian Learning, a neural plasticity mechanism. Hebb, who uses the nerve cell in his studies, investigated the interactions between the two nerve cells, and the rules he put forward formed the basis of the neural networks. This is now the recognized 'typical' rule used for unsupervised learning. Subsequently, computational machines called "calculators" were used as the first study to mimic a Hebbian network at MIT by Farley and Wesley A. Clark (1954).

In 1958, Frank Rosenblatt proposed a "perceptron pattern, an algorithm based on a two-tier computer learning network, using simple addition/subtraction operations for pattern recognition. Research in this area has long decelerated until hardware processing power increased after a study that showed that neural networks could not solve XOR (exclusive-or) problems and that there was not enough computer hardware capacity for large neural networks.

The backpropagation algorithm developed by Werbos in 1975 was able to solve the XOR problem effectively. A book written in the 1980s could fully explain the use of parallel distributed systems in the processing of neural networks. In 1982, John Hopfield of Caltech, in his paper presented to the National Academy of Sciences, described an approach not only to model brains but to create useful devices.

Openness and mathematical analysis have shown how artificial neural networks work and what they can do. In 1986, Rumelhart and McClelland wrote Parallel Distributed Processing (volumes I and II), a complete explosion took place in this area. In 1988, Neural Network, the first journal in the field, was founded by the International Association of Neural Networks (INNS).

After these years, research focusing on the development of neural networks has slowed down relatively. Because of the limitations of the processors, the process of learning neural networks takes weeks. For this reason, hardware developments were expected until 2000 years, and neural networks experienced a winter period. Hardware improvements then, shallow neural networks have been replaced by deep nets.

Applications of Deep Learning

Artificial neural networks are used in the solution of many different problems such as regression, classification, clustering, robotics, and control systems.

Areas of application include vehicle control, process control, system identification, trajectory prediction, natural resource management, playing, quantum chemistry, and decision making (backgammon, chess, poker), model identification (radar systems, face identification)-, data mining, visualization and e-mail spam filtering -. Also, artificial neural networks have been used to diagnose some types of cancer-.

In a project called ALVINN (Autonomous Land Vehicle In a Neural Network) for vehicle control, automatic driving at 20 km / h was achieved with a reverse propagation neural network trained by the reactions of a real driver. In another study, an artificial neural network was developed, which can predict future behavior (position, speed, and course) of ships. The developed model is intended to assist ship route planning, intensive port tariffs, and error detection.

In a study to control traffic flow, an artificial neural network technique was used to model and control highway traffic. While the developed system generates speed commands for every section of the lane vehicles need to follow to produce the 'traffic flow density distribution' required in the lane, is considered that it is possible to alleviate congestion and reduce human-induced errors by transmitting these commands to the drivers or directly to the control systems of the vehicles.

There are also studies using artificial neural networks in face recognition. In a study by Rowley et al., An automatic facial recognition system was presented. Automatic detection of eyes and mouth was monitored by spatial normalization of images, and classification of normalized images was performed by a hybrid (supervised and non-supervised) neural network.

In another article, a facial recognition system based on probabilistic decision-based neural networks (PDBNN) was proposed. The model performed recognition in 3 phases; first, the position of the human face was determined in the image, then significant features were removed from the positions of the two eyes, and the final step was completed by face recognition.

The article was run with FERET, ORL, and SCR datasets known in the field and produced successful results. The ability of neural networks to learn has been greatly enhanced by introducing restrictions from the task area. A study by Yann LeCun et al. shows how these constraints can be integrated into a backpropagation network through the architecture of the network. This approach has been successfully applied to the recognition of handwritten postal code numbers provided by the US Postal Service.

Artificial neural networks are also used for e-mail spam detection. SpamAssassin corpus in a study on the artificial neural network in the input layer changes have been made, the layers thought to work better, and the layers thought to be better replaced by the so-called CLA-ANN approach was tried. An algorithm has been developed for spam e-mails made with keywords. To detect such spam emails, hidden Markov models, and artificial neural networks were used to capture the statistical characteristics of spam variants of the same class.

Tested on the TREC 2007 dataset, it showed that the model was able to detect more than 90% of the spam content, and the false positive rate was below 13%. In another study, the anti-spam application was developed for agglutinative1 languages such as German. With the dynamic system established with artificial neural networks and Bayesian networks, user-specific filtering is performed. Roots extracted by the morphological analysis were classified, and 90% success was achieved in a data set with 750 mails.

Artificial neural networks, which are also used in cancer diagnosis, are very successful, especially in breast cancer. Breast screening (mammography) is a method used to diagnose breast cancer in the early stages. The mammogram can detect changes in the breast tissue that are too small to be noticed by the person or his physician. In a study, a neural network-based approach to the diagnosis of breast cancer was defined. The developed model aims to determine which woman is likely to suffer from a particular tumor type before starting mammography. The use of polynomial nuclei of support vector machines (SVM) has been tried in the actual clinical diagnosis of breast cancer. The test was conducted with new data, which was never used during the training and verification phase, and 100% accurate detection of cancer patients and 64% accurate diagnosis of cancer patients. So this

Deep Learning

Deep learning is a machine learning class. It uses many nonlinear processing unit layers for deep learning, feature extraction, and conversion. Each successive layer uses the output from the previous layer as input. Algorithms can be supervised (such as classification) or uncontrolled (such as pattern analysis). In deep learning, there is a structure based on learning multiple levels of representations of data. Top-level properties are derived from lower-level properties to form a hierarchical representation. In this representation, he learns multiple levels of representation that correspond to different levels of abstraction.

Deep learning is a method based on learning from the representation of data. Representation for an image; a vector of density values per pixel, or features such as edge clusters, custom shapes, may be considered. Some features represent the data better. Another advantage of deep learning is that it uses efficient algorithms for supervised / unsupervised property learning or hierarchical property extraction instead of handcrafted features.

The first general, learning algorithm for supervised deep-fed multilayer perceptions was published in 1965 by Ivakhnenko and Lapa. In this study, the best features of each layer are selected by statistical methods and transmitted to the next layer. Backpropagation was not used to train their networks end-to-end, the least-squares method was used from previous to subsequent layers

Fukushima proposed the first deep learning architecture Iv Neokognitron Sonra after Ivankhnenko in 1979. A self-organizing network has been developed with "teacherless learning" in the structure that is introduced from the visual nervous systems of vertebrates. Fukushima's nets included multiple bending and pond layers similar to modern nets.

The lack of learning in deep architectures was in the backpropagation of errors in multiple layers. Although backpropagation algorithms have been proposed in previous years, the first successful deep neural network application was developed by Yann LeCun. Although the network worked successfully, it was found to be unsuitable for practice as training lasted approximately three days. After this study, Yann LeCunn again applied the coiled backpropagation with the LeNet network to classify handwriting numbers (MNIST).

Using the wake-sleep algorithm developed jointly with Brendan Frey, Peter Dayan, and Geoffrey Hinton in 1995, they demonstrated that it is possible to train a network of six fully connected layers and hundreds of hidden layers, although the training lasts two days. Some important developments were made in 1997 for Hochreiter and Schmidhuber's recurrent neural networks, such as long short-term memory. Due to the cost of computing ANNs, despite their advantages, simpler models using problem-specific, hand-crafted features such as support vector machines have become a popular choice in the 1990s and 2000s.

Major improvements have been made with the faster operation of computers and later the installation of graphics processing units (GPUs). With faster computers and GPUs, the computational speed has increased 1000-fold over ten years. During this period, the neural network gradually began to rival support vector machines. In the context of ANN, the term "Deep Learning" was introduced in 2000 by Igor Aizenberg.

In an article published by Geoffrey Hinton in 2006, he demonstrated how the multilayer feedforward neural network could effectively train one layer at a time (trained each layer with an uncontrolled Boltzmann machine without supervision), and then fine-tune it with a controlled backpropagation method.

As GPU speeds increase, deep networks can be trained without prior training have used this approach in their deep network to win traffic signs, medical imaging, and character recognition competitions. Krizhevsky, Sutskever, and Hinton used a similar architecture in 2012. GPUs have been used to increase training speed and have proven efficacy using the normalized method called "dropout" 3, which has been developed in recent years to reduce overfitting in fully-connected layers. These approaches have brought them outstanding results in the ILSVRC-2012 ImageNet competition.

After these developments, technology firms such as Google, Facebook, and Microsoft realized this trend and started to invest in deep learning. Terrace

Deep Learning Architecture

There are many different types of deep learning architectures established by increasing the number of layers in artificial neural networks. In this section, the commonly used architectures will be briefly mentioned.

Convolutional Neural Networks

Convolutional Neural Networks (CNN or ConvNet) is a kind of multilayer sensors (MLP). The cells in the visual center were subdivided to cover the entire image. Simple cells concentrate on edge-like properties, while complex cells concentrate on the whole image with larger receptors. CNN, a forward-looking neural network, was inspired by the animals' visual center. The mathematical convolution process here can be considered as the response of a neuron to stimuli from its stimulus field.

The CNN consists of one or more convolutional layers, subsampling layers followed by one or more fully connected layers such as a standard multilayer neural network. One benefit of CNNs is that they have fewer training and fewer parameters than networks that are fully connected to the same number of hidden units. The input in a convolutional layer is a picture of m x m x r. Where m is the height and width of the image, respectively, and r is the number of channels (for example, r = 3 in an RGB image).

The convolutional layer consists of k filters with dimensions n x n x q. For the filter, the q value selected is usually the same as the value of n, and r (channel), which is smaller than the size of the image. With these filters, k produces locally linked feature maps, each m-n + 1 m-n + 1. Then, for each map, a p x p downsampling process (p-value, usually between 2-5 according to image size) is applied with maximum or average pooling, such as the example in.

LeNet's architecture was the first CNN network, introduced in 1988 by Yann LeCun and improvements continued until 1998.

In the LeNet network, the lower layers consist of consecutive layered convolution and maximum pooling layers. The subsequent upper layers correspond to the traditional MLP, which is fully linked.

CNN algorithms are applied in many different fields, such as natural language processing and biomedical, especially in the field of image and audio processing. State-of-the-art results have been achieved, especially in these fields. On the MNIST dataset, Cireşan has succeeded in reducing the error rate by up to 2% with CNN. In another study on MNIST and NORB datasets, it was stated that the learning process took place very fast, and it was the most successful method until the time it was published. In 2014, in the ImageNet Large Scale Visual Recognition Competition, millions of images and hundreds of object classes, and the teams that achieved the most successful ratings for object classification and detection, all used the CNN algorithms.

In 2015, a multi-layer CNN demonstrated the ability to capture faces in wide-angle ranges, including reverse faces. This network has been trained on a database of 200,000 images with faces in various angles and directions and 20 million images without faces.

CNN models are effective for various NLP problems. Excellent results were obtained in semantic decomposition, search query acquisition, sentence modeling, classification, and prediction problems.

CNN algorithms have also been used in drug discovery. AtomNet, developed by Atomwise in 2015, was the first deep neural network developed for drug design. Trained with 3D representations of chemical reactions, the system has been used to discover new biomolecules in diseases such as Ebola and sclerosis.

CNN was also used for the Go game, and the GNU Go algorithm, which was developed by traditional methods, was defeated by a pre-trained 12-layer CNN algorithm in 97% of the games. Developed by Google DeepMind, CNN-based AlphaGo was the first time a professional human-defeating program.

Recurrent Neural Network

Jeff Elman designed the Simple Recurring Network (SRN). For each word used in Elman's sentence structure simulation, the average pattern clustering on hidden patterns is separated from the noun and verb categories.

Also, live-inanimate distinctions between the names, even man-animal, hunter-predator clusters between animals are separated.

RNNs are neural networks where connections form directed loops between different units. This cycle creates a network internal state, allowing the network to display dynamic temporal behavior. An RNN will process random input sequences using input memory, different behavior to the feedforward networks.

Long Short Term Memory

There is an approach based on the use of prior knowledge in RNN architectures. For example, it is easy to guess the word "soil indie in the sentence" "Tree grows in soil." But when the inter-context gap increases, RNN is difficult to use information from the past.

While predicting the word "English indie in a text such as, it can be predicted that it will be a language name based on the sentence it contains, but it is necessary to keep the sentence at the beginning of the text in memory to predict the correct word. The "long-term dependencies that are possible in theory have turned out to cause major problems in practice.

To solve this problem, a special type of RNN, Long Short Term Memory Networks (LSTM), which can learn long term dependencies, was introduced by Hochreiter and Schmidhuber in 1997.

The LSTM architecture has three gates, input, forgetting, and output 3, block input, a single cell (Constant Fault Loop), an output activation function, and peephole connections. The output of the block is repeatedly connected to the input of the block and all of its doors. Surveillance links and forgetting gates are not included in the first developed architecture. A forgetting gate has been added to reset the LSTM's own status, and surveillance links have been added to make it easier to learn precise timings.

LSTM architectures provide very good results in speech/text processing. In the frame-based voice classification study, the TIMIT dataset containing rich content in different dialects was used, and a success rate of 70% was achieved. Another LSTM approach, which underwent end-to-end training with appropriate adjustments, achieved a success rate of 83% on the same dataset.

In another study, an accuracy rate of 84.5% was given on the Verbmobil data set, which contained extensive speech data in keyword detection. In another study, a deep model using fully automated CNN and LSTM algorithms that learn to classify human activities without prior knowledge has been successfully implemented.

Another interesting application is the composition of music with LSTM. In this study, a model has been designed to show that LSTM can successfully learn music in a blues genre and create new compositions in this style with long-term learning ability.

LSTM architectures have also been used in a wide range of subjects, such as detection of protein homology independent of alignment, designing a system that learns to tie nodes in robotic heart surgery, learning in irregular languages , and offline handwriting recognition.

Restricted (Deep) Boltzmann Machines

The restricted Boltzmann machine (RBM) was first introduced in 1986 under the name Harmonium, but Geoffrey Hinton et al introduced it. In 2006 as a rapid learning algorithm. RBM is a productive random, artificial neural network that can learn probability distribution on the input set. RBM is a type of Boltzmann Machines.

They are composed of two-part graphs with symmetrical connections between them, visible and hidden. The nodes in a graph do not have a connection between them. In contrast, there are connections between unrestricted Boltzmann machines and hidden units which have more effective training algorithms compared to the general class of Boltzmann machines.

RBMs are a useful algorithm for different topics such as size reduction, classification, collaborative filtering, feature learning, and topic modeling.

Deep Belief Networks

Deep belief networks (DBN), introduced by Geoffrey Hinton, and are defined as the heap of RBMs given in the previous section. Each RBM layer is linked to both the previous and subsequent layers. However, the nodes of any layer do not have horizontal communication with each other. It is capable of grading with a softmax layer as the last layer or clustering for independent learning.

- When X is accepted as input data which is a sequence of property vectors, the learning process in a DBN network is performed by the following steps;

- To obtain the weight matrix, an RBM on X is trained, and W weights are obtained. This (W) is used as the weight matrix between the two lower layers of the web.

- By sampling or calculating the average activation of hidden nodes, the RBM converts the new data X 'sequence, which is input for the next layer X.

- The conversion $X \leftarrow X$ 'is repeated until it reaches the top two times of the network.

- For all parameters of this deep architecture, the DBN probability is fine-tuned according to a proxy.

DBN architectures have been applied to image recognition and production. In another study, word-number vectors were obtained in a large document dataset with a system using DBN instead of applying

TF-IDF to the whole document. To describe human motion, Taylor et al. Have synthesized various sequences of motion and provided online data display of lost data during motion capture.

Deep Auto-Encoders

Auto-encoders (AE), called the diablo network, is a special artificial neural network used for uncontrolled learning. AE aims to learn a representation (coding) for size reduction for a dataset. In recent years, the AE concept has become more widely used to learn productive models of data. AE is a feedforward neural network that roughly aims to learn the best features from the compressed representation of input data.

Deep or stacked auto-encoders (DAE) are the neural network of multiple layers of AEs, where the outputs on each layer are connected to the inputs of the consecutive layer.

In the first hidden layer, the Input I sequence was encrypted. The sequence of properties obtained in the next hidden layer as input and the feature II sequence was obtained as a result of the encryption. The feature II sequence was given as input to the softmax classifier in the last layer as the feature vector, and the classification was performed with this vector.

DAE architecture has been applied for fabric defect detection, and the deep network formed by two consecutive AEs has achieved very successful features. Mail for spam capture

In another study, the results were compared with other methods such as Naive Bayes, Support Vector Machines, Decision Trees, and showed better performance in both accuracy and f1 measurements. In a study on speech spectrogram coding, a DAE-based architecture was applied, and it was observed that the speech data and the results obtained were approximately the same as the success achieved for encoding image patches.

Deep Learning Practices

In the previous section, an analysis was made through the architectures. Here, differentiation will be made on a subject-by-topic basis, which will focus on which methods are applied to which area in recent years.

Natural Language Processing

Deep learning algorithms, especially DAE, LSTM, CNN architectures, which are quite successful in the field of natural language processing, have produced impressive results. Emotion analysis with a small amount of tagged data is a known problem. Shusen Zhou, a semi-educated learning algorithm called Active Deep Network (ADN), has worked on this problem. The RBM-based deep network was applied on five emotion analysis datasets.

In another study on emotion analysis, a two-stage semi-educative learning method called fuzzy DBN is presented. First, it was trained with the data set generated by semi-educated learning with DBN. Then, a fuzzy membership function based on the views learned by the deep architecture came into play, and effective results were obtained compared to previous studies. Another study inspired by emotion analysis used the RNN model, a new deep learning-based network that classifies short messages (safe and insecure) for automatic security auditing of short messages in prisons. Typical features are extracted from short messages by word2vec and classified by RNN.

Experimental results have shown that the RNN model achieves an average accuracy of 92.7%, which is higher than that of SVM. Sentence classification is an important problem in natural language processing. With a CNN-based approach, pre-trained word vectors have been used in the sentence classification problem and have achieved high success on seven highly valued topics (including emotion analysis and question classification). In addition, the CNN method was used for multi-tasking learning. RNN networks are also used in studies on voice recognition.

In a study of text summarization, with DAE, a single document summarizing methods for calculating a property field from the Term Frequency (tf) input is presented. An ensemble-based learning method called ENAE, with random noise added to tf values, was tried. E-mail data sets on two different subjects have been studied, and average recall values of 11.2% have been achieved. An LSTM-based approach to identifying keywords in texts has been compared to HMM that has been successful in this area and is more successful.

In a study to determine the gender of the author, CNN and LSTM were used together. The study of Russian texts has shown close success to state-of-art studies with an accuracy of 86% compared with traditional methods. In a study on the validation of authorship, the use of DBN was investigated. The model has lexical, syntactic, and application-specific features. The model tested on the Twitter and Enron e-mail dataset showed promise with error rates of 8-16%.

Obtaining low-dimensional semantic representations in texts or queries obtained over the web is an important problem for data processing. CLSM (Convolutional Latent Semantic Model) is a large scale real-world data that is trained with click data from web pages. Document ranking evaluation has been made, and it is seen that the outstanding semantic information in the documents is obtained, and it is superior to the previous methods. In the study of Jianfeng Gao, a CNN-based deep semantic similarity model (DSSM) is presented to recommend a user of interest-based on the source document he read.

DSSM has received training on millions of Web migrations and matched source-to-target document pairs to feature vectors. In this way, the distances between the source documents and the documents that may be of interest have been reduced. The model was not only successful in the field of interestingness but also produced effective results in subject modeling. Other similar approaches to semantic decomposition have been applied. The correct expression of sentences is important for understanding the language. In a study conducted with the CNN method, semantic modeling of sentences was studied and showed a serious success with 25% error rates.

In the natural language processing area, the user's words should be labeled differently according to the concept/area. In one study, although the data were similar, an approach was proposed to take advantage of the available annotation when the label data sets were different. This approach is based on label insertions from CCA (canonical correlation analysis). When the results were examined, significant similarities such as as-calendar-reminder.

In another study, the model developed using CNN on the image and bidirectional RNN algorithms on the sentences to add the appropriate identifiers to the correct regions in the image data were applied on Flickr8K, Flickr30K, and MSCOCO datasets. The descriptors produced on the region level and the full image were found to be quite accurate. Again, the same problem is solved with similar models on other data sets. Mail spam detection has also been used in the field of deep learning in recent years. In a study conducted with the DAE method, the model gave much better results than the traditional methods.

Studies on speech recognition with the DBN model have yielded impressive results on voice recording data.

Image / Video Processing

One of the most popular problems in image processing is the image classification problem. As a common set of assessments for this task, MNIST was used. MNIST consists of 60000 for education and 10000 handwriting for testing. Numerous methods have been tested on this dataset, ranging from artificial neural networks to statistical methods. The most successful result to date

This is the study of Ciresan in 2012 with 0.23 errors. In this study using the CNN model, width normalization was applied as a pretreatment. Also, in 2011, the CNN approach achieved superhuman performance for the first time in the visual pattern recognition competition.

Also, the ICDAR Chinese handwriting competition was won in 2011 and the ISBI painting division competition in May 2012. In October 2012, a similar system, created by Alex Krizhevsky, Geoffrey Hinton, and his team, won the large-scale ImageNet competition with a marked difference in shallow machine learning methods.

A similar model has also won ICPR and MICCAI competitions for the analysis of large medical images for cancer detection. In 2014, the error rate in the ImageNet competition, which uses deep learning, was further reduced using similar deep learning models. In addition, deep learning-based uncontrolled learning algorithms are used to extract class-specific features from unlabeled data.

In a study, pooling and normalization combined with a 9-layer DAE and a data set with 10 million images downloaded from the Internet were trained. The training was carried out in 3 days with a parallel cluster formed with 1000 machines (16,000 cores). With this model, it is possible to identify the face recognition system without face labeling, even cat face and human body part.

Deep learning algorithms are also very successful for object recognition problems. A study using deep residual networks (ILSVRC 2015) ranked first in ImageNet detection, ImageNet localization, and COCO segmentation competitions. In another study, to identify the objects in the image and to make semantic segmentation, rich features were obtained with the algorithm called R-CNN, where regions and CNN are combined. The problem of scene labeling can be solved by labeling raw pixels in an image with the object category to which they belong.

Clement Farabet and his team proposed a multiscale CNN model. SIFT Flow, Barcelona, Stanford produced much faster and more successful results on background data sets than other approaches. The detection of pedestrians is an important problem. The uncontrolled learning method developed with the sparse CNN model has yielded competitive results.

Biomedical Image / Information Processing

Since deep learning can be considered as a sub-branch of image processing, medical image analysis is also very effective in solving problems. In brain tumor research, image segmentation is needed. For this task, automatic segmentation has been successfully performed in recent years with deep learning methods. Deep learning models have enabled objective interpretations, especially with large amounts of MRI data.

CNN-based algorithms, especially for automated MRI segmentation for brain tumors, have produced successful results with distinctive features and other segmentation problem. MRI images were also performed for these diseases. In a study, low area knee MRI scans were applied to the segmentation of tibial cartilage, and 114 have been tested on invisible screening.

A deep learning model was established for the detection of benign and malignant tumors from images obtained from SWE (share wave elastography), which is an important parameter in breast cancer clinical computer diagnosis. RBM and PGBM (point-wise gated Boltzmann Machine) 2-layer model created with 227 SWE data trained, 93.4% showed accuracy.

In another study, deep learning using auto-extracted features in lung cancer detection was compared with the CADx system using traditional (manually) extracted features. A deep learning network has been established with three channels, including CNN, DBN, and DAE. When the results were examined according to the AUC (area under the curve), CNN was significantly superior to CADx, DBN was close but superior, and DAE showed worse results.

It is a big problem for the pharmaceutical industry that the candidate drugs cannot be released to the market due to negative consequences. These failures in chemical compounds are due to inadequate efficacy, incorrect reaction with non-target compounds, or unexpected toxic effects. In 2012, with the multitasking deep neural network, George Dahl and his team won a competition called om Merck Molecular Activity Problem on bimolecular target prediction of the compound. In 2014, Sepp Hochreiter and his team won a competition to identify off-target and toxic effects in drugs using deep learning again. These and similar developments have shown that deep learning can be superior to virtual scanning.

In 2015, AtomNet, which used deep learning for structure-based drug design, was launched by Atomwise and was subsequently used to discover new candidate biomolecules for diseases such as Ebola and sclerosis.

Disclosure of genetic information is an important problem for bioinformatics. A DAE-based solution was proposed to solve this problem and produced better results than standard machine learning methods. In another study, LSTM was applied to a well-known criterion for the detection of distant protein homology, which should be classified as belonging to a SCOP superfamily of a protein.

Although it gives close values in terms of accuracy compared to other approaches with similar classification performance for model classification, it is relatively fast for them. It is important to know the sequencing properties of DNA and RNA binding proteins to develop regulatory process models in biological systems and to identify causal disease variables. In a study, it has been successfully used with a deep learning model that offers a scalable, flexible, and unified computational approach to pattern discovery of sequence properties.

Other Applications

The most common application areas are given in the above section. Also, it was observed that deep learning methods were applied in different fields.

In a study for sleep quality prediction, some deep learning methods (CNN, RNN, LSTM, etc.) were compared with the predictors' performance of traditional logistic regression. The CNN algorithm gave the best results. In addition, deep learning algorithms have been applied to subjects such as human activity recognition and human motion detection.

A deep reinforcement learning method has been tried in CRM (Customer Relationship Management) automation. The neural network has been used to approximate the value of possible direct marketing actions in customer status areas defined in terms of RFM (actuality-frequency-amount) variables.

DARPA has created the Deep Research and Text Filtering (DEFT) program to utilize the power of natural language processing. This artificial intelligence has the potential to enable defense analysts to search for large-scale documents efficiently and may disclose the implicit expression of activity (abnormality detection) in these documents.

Deep learning applications such as autonomous vehicle systems and multimedia management are also being tried, and improvements are expected in the coming years. Deep learning cards and supercomputers produced by NVIDIA are being run for these goals.

Intelligent traffic planning is an important factor in the establishment of smart cities. Overcoming nonlinear and random features in the transport network is a major challenge. In a study, a deep learning model called DeepSense was used to train traffic GPS data to estimate traffic flow. With the proposed model, a 5% improvement was achieved according to existing methods. In another study, traffic congestion modeling using RBM was studied.

Indoor orientation is an important problem. In a study, a quadcopter was proposed to be able to walk independently indoors and to find a target (e.g., a bag) using a single camera. The CNN algorithm simulates the action selection of an expert pilot and demonstrates system performance in real-time experiments in various indoor environments.

Summary
As explained in the previous sections, deep learning algorithms are used in many areas and problems. With the increasing amount of data, especially in image processing, there are problems such as image classification and object recognition. In competitions such as ILSVRC, deep learning methods that prove itself as a method to cope with big data are frequently used and give the most successful results.

Also, autonomous vehicle technologies use real-time data processing capabilities and GPU-based deep learning algorithms. To cope with the data from the vehicles 4-5 cameras and many sensors, deep learning seems to be a way to be used in the future.

One of the most important problems of big data is the cost of labeling. To overcome this, uncontrolled deep learning methods such as AE will come to the fore again in the future.

Another remarkable area is natural language processing and sound processing. Deep learning algorithms combine image processing with natural language processing, especially in image tagging and segmenting, adding titles to images. Almost all teams engaged in research on deep learning make improvements in this area.

It is considered that deep learning algorithms (especially RNN, LSTM, CNN) will be used successfully in solving problems such as text summarizing and classification in natural language processing.

In line with this aim, a study will be conducted to solve problems such as extracting topics from texts, identifying keywords, and developing question and answer systems. The data set to be used in the study consists of the text of the operator-customer interviews of a call center. To solve these problems, deep learning methods and statistical-based methods will be used together.

Chapter Two

DEEP LEARNING IN
PRACTICEWITH PYTHON

The most interesting thing about this "modern fever" for Machine Learning -or Deep Learning more specifically- is that it is within everyone's reach, unlike what we have seen previously, where we have realized the great difficulties encountered in the advancement of this branch of Artificial Intelligence in the mid to late last century.

When it comes to design and software, there is a strong Deep Learning community within the world of free software to empower and implement solutions and projects at these levels. Development languages such as R, C++, or Python are increasingly fed by community-engineered libraries to achieve significant advances in Machine Learning, which translates into great solutions spanning language processing, speech recognition, computer vision, data mining, or the Internet of things.

In this chapter, we have chosen to work with the Python programming language, as well as being a high-level language of free nature and a certain ease at the time of implementation, allows us to make use of almost a hundred libraries oriented to automatic and deep learning.

Throughout this chapter, we will present different works and examples of projects in which we have worked to understand the inner workings of automatic and deep learning in practice.

Getting Started with Theano

The first stop on our way to use Deep Learning using Python takes us to Theano.

Developed by researchers at the University of Montreal, Canada, Theano is a powerful Python mathematical library that allows us to define, optimize and evaluate expressions involving multi-dimensional matrices, being very useful for us when designing artificial neural networks and obtaining greater efficiency in very large calculations. Theano also enables symbolic definitions and fully transparent use of GPU processors.

 Two exciting features of this library are the shared variables and the update parameters. The former called shared variables, are a hybrid between symbolic and nonsymbolic variables, whose values can be shared among various functions. These shared variables can be used in symbolic expressions such as the return of objects in an array. They also have an internal value that defines the value taken by this symbolic variable in all the functions used.

The other great feature is the update parameter of Theano functions. These updates must be supplied in a list of tuples in the form {shared variable, new expression}, but it can also be a dictionary. The object of all this is that each time this function is executed, the value of each shared variable will be replaced by the result of the corresponding expression.

Classification of MNIST Digits using Theano

The first project carried out with Theano would be to classify a series of handwritten digit images using the logistic regression classification method, using artificial neural networks and the well-known MNIST digit database. This database is made up of around 60,000 handwritten digit images -and another 10,000 images for testing- consisting of images of the same in grayscale.

This logistic regression is a probabilistic and linear classifier. An input vector is projected into a series of hyperplanes, each corresponding to a class, to create the classification.

The distance between the hyperplane and the entrance indicates the probability of the entrance belonging to one class or another class. Loss function must be minimized so the right model parameters may be learned. Where logistic regression is concerned, using the negative likelihood ratio as the loss in the most common method. And for the loss function, the minimization algorithm is the stochastic descending gradient, together with mini-batches.

The neural network to be built will be modeled using a multi-layer perception, with a total of 784 inputs (one per pixel of each image: 28x28), 110 hidden layers, and a total of 10 outputs. Each one of these outputs corresponds to a digit from 0 to 9, which only one of these inputs will be activated to 1 indicating which is the handwritten number that has been passed through the network input, once it has been trained — a total of 1.00 with a learning index of 0.13.

Among the different objectives to determine the problem of classification of digits of the MNIST database are:

- The creation and behavior of the class that will perform the logistic regression, which incorporates different tensors that will act as input and output units of the network, including their weight matrices and error prediction methods for each example of the network, all through shared Theano variables. Among the methods defined in this class is the calculation of the negative likelihood ratio to minimize the loss function and a method that is responsible for representing the number of total errors on the number of total examples.

- Learning and training of the previously defined network model, in charge of minimizing the network cost function and updating the weight matrix of the entire data set. With Theano, this is done in a relatively simple way since, with the functions of Theano itself and the parameters of updates of them, it allows us to specify in only a couple of commands how to update the parameters of the model using a list of tuples.

- Network testing, in charge of recovering the number of examples of the network that have not managed to be classified by the model. For this, a Theano function is used that calculates the errors that are made in a mini-batch -or example- of the set of tests, being compared with that of the validation set.

At the exit, we will visualize information regarding the percentage of error of each epoch on each image of each digit, including the one of better validation and the speed of computation of the network using the chosen model.

Pylearn2

Training a neural network using Theano requires a high level of complexity, since it is our obligation to define implicitly how the model to be used will behave, what learning algorithms to use and implement them in situ, define and implement the appropriate cost function for each problem, train each example of our set of tests by hand and check-in each case if it has been classified by the model correctly or not.

That's why there are other Python libraries based on Machine Learning that allow us to place a higher abstraction layer and simplify the processes of experimentation with neural networks for a given problem. One of these libraries is Pylearn2, which is the other great Python library that has been used in this End-of-Grade Project.

Pylearn2 uses Theano internally and allows us to divide Machine Learning problems into three distinct parts: the dataset with the sample dataset, the model used for the network, and the training algorithms used to train the model. In this way, the training algorithm works to adapt the model to the values expected in the data set.

All this information is collected in a YAML file, a document marking language. Pylearn2 supports almost thirty datasets, highlighting some such as MNIST, CIFAR10, CSV Dataset or Sparse Dataset, and its syntax in YAML for these datasets is as follows:

```
dataset: &train
!obj:pylearn2.datasets.csv_dataset.CSVDataset { # Dataset attributes

},
```

The list of Deep Learning models that can support Pylearn2 is also very varied, highlighting MLP, K-Means, RBM, Autoencoder or Softmax Regression. Its syntax would be as follows:

```
model: !obj:pylearn2.models.mlp.MLP { # Model attributes

layers: [ !obj:pylearn2.models.mlp.ConvRectifiedLinear { # A layer of convolutional neurons

},

!obj:pylearn2.models.mlp.MLP {
```

```
# A layer formed by a multi-layered perceptron

},

!obj:pylearn2.models.mlp.Softmax {

# An output layer with Softmax activation function

}

],

},
```

When it comes to training algorithms, diversity is much scarcer, with the two main ones standing out: Stochastic Gradient Descent and Batch Gradient Descent. Your YAML syntax:

```
algorithm: !obj:pylearn2.training_algorithms.sgd.SGD { #
Algorithm attributes

},
```

Broadly speaking, these are the three main components of a YAML file, although it is possible to add extra information such as instructions for preprocessing dataset data, the neural network learning index, the network cost minimization functions, monitoring any attributes immersed in the YAML file as the network is being trained, or exporting graphs of special relevance during training.

As we can see, the complexity index with respect to Theano decreases enormously, since we only have to worry about filling in this YAML configuration file to specify the type of network we want, abstracting from how to implement all these functions in Python -it really does everything Theano internally- without really programming a single line of code.

To train the network, besides this YAML configuration file we need the Python file that will take care of the training itself, called train.py, which is a file that Pylearn2 already brings when installing the library and is generic for any network that we believe so, except in very specific cases, it is not necessary to edit it.

CIFAR10 using Pylearn2

In the practical case in which it has been worked for the making of contact with Pylearn2, it has been used another well-known database of images used habitually in problems of Machine Learning: the CIFAR10. This database contains more than 80 million small 32-pixel color images classified into different categories.

Once with the data dataset, which can be downloaded from its official page, we proceed to train the model as marked in its corresponding YAML file, which is where our neural network will be described and configured.

The model used to train it is the RBM, a Boltzmann Restricted Gaussian Machine, based on a recurrent neural network. A total of 192 input neurons (test images of 8x8 pixels and three channels of different colors), 400 neurons in their hidden layers, and a learning index of 0.1 were used. The reduction in image size is because the larger the net entry, the more weights to train, and the slower the whole training process.

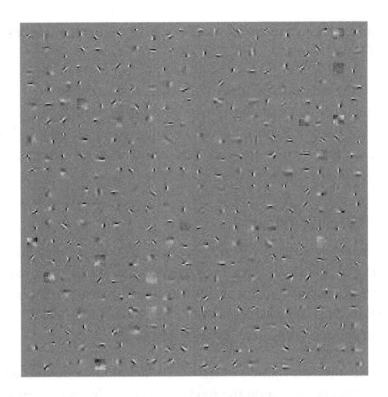

Visualization of the training weights with CIFAR10.

As a result of the training, inspecting the final model with the weights obtained after it, we can visualize the first approach for the identification of the given images after only four periods, and the classification error rate of each image has been reflected in 28%.

```
Parameter and initial learning rate summary:
        W: 0.1
        bias_vis: 0.1
        bias_hid: 0.1
        sigma_driver: 0.1
Compiling sgd_update...
Compiling sgd_update done. Time elapsed: 27.923031 seconds
compiling begin_record_entry...
compiling begin_record_entry done. Time elapsed: 0.051031 seconds
Monitored channels:
        bias_hid_max
        bias_hid_mean
        bias_hid_min
        bias_vis_max
        bias_vis_mean
        bias_vis_min
        h_max
        h_mean
        h_min
        learning_rate
        objective
        reconstruction_error
        total_seconds_last_epoch
```

Starting the training process.

```
Monitoring step:
        Epochs seen: 4
        Batches seen: 120000
        Examples seen: 600000
        bias_hid_max: -0.119526364371
        bias_hid_mean: -2.18671616478
        bias_hid_min: -3.24759610714
        bias_vis_max: 0.199195119615
        bias_vis_mean: -0.000157558304656
        bias_vis_min: -0.141461366806
        h_max: 0.466855162051
        h_mean: 0.0439254012314
        h_min: 0.00639914518957
        learning_rate: 0.1
        objective: 3.2779371318
        reconstruction_error: 28.4721905224
        total_seconds_last_epoch: 72.1537
        training_seconds_this_epoch: 57.800005
monitoring channel is objective
growing learning rate to 0.101000
Saving to cifar_grbm_smd.pkl...
Saving to cifar_grbm_smd.pkl done. Time elapsed: 0.121924 seconds
Saving to cifar_grbm_smd.pkl...
Saving to cifar_grbm_smd.pkl done. Time elapsed: 0.075991 seconds
```

End of the training process after four epochs.

Getting Started with TensorFlow

TensorFlow is a numerical operation library created by Google, which is used as the bottom layer of deep learning. This chapter includes:

- TensorFlow introduction

- How to define, compile and evaluate expressions with TensorFlow

- How to ask for help

Note: TensorFlow does not currently support Windows. You can use Docker or a virtual machine. Windows users can skip this chapter.

What is TensorFlow?

TensorFlow is an open-source mathematical computing engine created by Google and released under the Apache 2.0 protocol. TF's API is Python, but the underlying is C ++. Unlike Theano, TF takes into account both industry and research and uses it in projects such as RankBrain, DeepDream. TF can be used in a single CPU or GPU, mobile devices, and large-scale distributed systems.

Install TensorFlow

TF supports Python 2.7 and 3.3 and above. Installation is simple:

sudo pip install TensorFlow

Enough.

TensorFlow Example

The calculation of TF is represented graphically:

- Node: A node performs calculations and has one or more inputs and outputs. The data between nodes is called a tensor: a multidimensional array of real numbers.

- Edge: A graph that defines data, branches, loops, and overlays, as well as advanced operations, such as waiting for a calculation to complete.

- Action: Take an input value and get an output value; for example, add, subtract, multiply, and divide.

Simple TensorFlow

Let's talk briefly about TensorFlow: we define two floating-point variables a and b, define an expression (c − a + b), turn the expression into a function, compile, and calculate:

```
import tensorflow as tf

# declare two symbolic floating-point scalars

a = tf.placeholder(tf.float32)

b = tf.placeholder(tf.float32)

# create a simple symbolic expression using the add function
add = tf.add(a, b)

# bind 1.5 to 'a', 2.5 to 'b', and evaluate 'c'

sess = tf.Session()

binding = {a: 1.5, b: 2.5}

c = sess.run(add, feed_dict=binding)

print(c)
```

The result is 4: 1.5 + 2.5 = 4.0. Large matrix operations are similar.

Other Deep Learning Models

TensorFlow comes with many models that can be called directly: First, look at the installation location of TensorFlow:

```
python -c 'import os; import inspect; import TensorFlow; print (os.path.dirname (inspect.getfile (TensorFlow)))'
```

The results are similar to:

/usr/lib/python2.7/site-packages/TensorFlow

Enter the directory; you can see many examples:

- Multi-threaded word2vec mini-batch Skip-Gram model

- Multi-threaded word2vec Skip-Gram model

- CNN model of CIFAR-10

- LeNet-5-like end-to-end MNIST model

- An end-to-end model with an attention mechanism

The example directory contains examples of the MNIST dataset. The TensorFlow website is also helpful, including different networks and datasets. TensorFlow also has a web version that you can experiment with directly.

- TensorFlow, like Theano, is a numerical computing library

- TensorFlow can develop models directly like Theano

- TensorFlow is better than Theano's packaging

Now we will study Keras: we use this library to develop deep learning models.

Getting Started with Keras

Python's scientific computing packages are mainly Theano and TensorFlow: very powerful, but a bit difficult to use. Keras can easily build neural networks based on one of these two packages. This chapter includes:

- Deep learning with Keras

- How to configure Keras backend

- Keras common operations

let us start.

What is Keras?

Keras can build deep learning models based on Theano or TensorFlow for easy research and development. Keras can run on Python 2.7 or 3.5 and painlessly call back-end CPU or GPU networks. Keras was developed by Google's Francois Chollet and followed these principles:

- Modularity: Each module is a separate process or diagram, and all problems of deep learning can be solved by assembling modules

- Simplification: Provides the easiest way to solve problems without decoration, maximizing readability

- Scalability: the addition of new modules is particularly easy to experiment with new ideas

- Python: Do not use any native format, only native Python

Installing Keras

Keras is well installed, but you need to install at least one of Theano or TensorFlow.

Install Keras using PyPI:

sudo pip install Keras

The following sentence can be seen in the version of Keras:

python -c "import keras; print keras.__version__."

Python displays the version number of Keras, for example:

1.0.1

Keras upgrade is also a sentence:

sudo pip install --upgrade keras

Configuring Keras Backend

Keras is a lightweight API for Theano and TensorFlow, so it must be used with the backend. Backend configuration requires only one file:

~/.keras/keras.json

Inside is:

{"epsilon": 1e-07, "floatx": "float32", "backend": "theano"}

The default backend is theano; it can be changed to TensorFlow. The following command will display the backend of Keras:

python -c "from keras import backend; print backend._BACKEND."

The default will be displayed:

Using Theano backend.

theano

Variables KERAS_BACKENDcan control the back end of Keras, for example:

KERAS_BACKEND=tensorflow python -c "from keras import backend; print backend._BACKEND."

Will output:

Using TensorFlow backend.

tensorflow

Building Deep Learning Models with Keras

Keras' goal is to build models. The main model is Sequential: the overlay of different layers. After the model is created, it can be compiled, and the back-end can be called for optimization, and the loss function and optimization algorithm can be specified.

The compiled model needs to import data: you can add the data in batches, or you can add all at once. All calculations are performed in this step. The trained model can then make predictions or classifications. The general steps are:

1. Define the model: create the Sequential model and add each layer

2. Compiling the model: Specifying the loss function and optimization algorithm, using the model compile()method

3. Fitting the data: using the model's fit()method to fit the data

4. Prediction: using models evaluate()or predict()methods for predicting

- Keras is a wrapper for Theano and TensorFlow, reducing complexity

- Keras is a minimal, modular package that can get started quickly

- Keras can build models by definition-compile-fit and make predictions

Next Chapter

This is the forefront of Python machine learning: in the next project, we will build a machine learning environment on the cloud step by step.

Chapter Three

STUDY AND IMPLEMENTATION OF NEURAL NETWORKS USING PYLEARN2

Once we have worked on some practical examples proposed by two of the technologies that allow us to implement deep learning techniques, it is time to proceed to build our neural networks making use of the knowledge acquired in the previous chapters. In this way, a small final study will be elaborated where different types of models and techniques used in Deep Learning will be analyzed, detailing which of these techniques or models turn out to be more favorable for the set of data with which we are working, depending on different parameters of the network.

For this project, we will make use of the Pylearn2 library since it allows us to parameterize the network and show us the results of the training of the network in the function of numerous variables.

Data Set

To train our network, we will need information or sets of data to deal with in the entry of the same. This dataset comes from the Kaggle platform, a non-profit website that establishes "challenges" for its users related to Big Data and Machine Learning, and in which we can find hundreds of datasets for processing.

The selected data dataset, in CSV format, will be made up of 418 entries corresponding to passengers who took part in the Titanic journey, each of them having information such as their name, age, sex, the port of embarkation, travel ticket or the class in which they were travelling.

With the set of data in our power, before proceeding to build and train the network, we must parameterize some of the data of this dataset. Given that some qualitative variables do not influence the training of neural networks (name, surname, travel ticket or port of embarkation), we will proceed to eliminate some of these data (name and surname) and replace the rest with numeric variables that do add more value to our data.

Parameterization in Pylearn

Once parameterized our input data, we will do the same with Pylearn2.

The treatment of an input CSV file in Pylearn2 is done using a CSVDataset class, defined in the csv_dataset.py file of the library itself. Our task will be to overwrite this class -rename it as CSVDataset2- adjusting it to the characteristics of our CSV file.

This class will have essential parameters for the treatment of our CSV file, such as the path where our data file is located, if headers are included in the data, the delimiter character of each data, or from which data to start reading.

Also, by default, CSVDataset works with the loadtxt() method of the Numpy class to read each data from the CSV file, so that it is necessary to specify for each header of our file what type of data it is and its length, making use of Numpy data types objects.

To avoid this, after trying unsuccessfully to parameterize our dataset with the appropriate data types, it was finally decided to opt for an alternative to the loadtxt() method, the also genfromtxt() method, whose functionality is similar to the previous one but where it is not necessary to explicitly specify the type of data being read from the dataset, as well as its length, performing this method dynamically.

With these slight modifications, we are now ready to build our neural network and its training file.

Neural Construction

Once the data is ready, it's time to take full advantage of the potential provided by Pylearn2 to build and model our first neural network and establish the guidelines selected for your training.

Pylearn2 has two systems for modeling a neural network and its associated training: well establishing all the mechanisms of the network that we want to dispose directly on a Python file or - in a much less expensive way - building a YAML file of configuration of the network, where to be able to parameterize with many fewer lines of code the network and our system of training. We will opt for this last option.

The next step will be to decide which architecture we are going to build for our network, adjusting it to the data that we know we have to pass to the entrance of the same one. As we have seen in previous chapters, YAML files allow us to configure a network and its training by establishing three main characteristics: the dataset is chosen, the neural network model selected and the training algorithm applied to the data according to the model chosen.

The dataset has already been decided because since we will work with a CSV file, we will take as a dataset in this YAML an object of type CSV Dataset. In it, we will detail some parameters such as the path where our CSV file is located; we will indicate that we will classify the data instead of regression, that our first row of data will be their headers and that our data delimiter value will be commas.

```
dataset: &train
!obj:pylearn2.datasets.csv_dataset2.CSVDataset2 { path:
'test.csv',

    task:

    'classification',

    expect_headers:

    True,

    delimiter:

    ',',

    },
```

The next step is to decide the architectural model of the network to be used. In order not to complicate ourselves excessively, we will opt for the most common model of artificial neural networks of which we have already spoken at length previously: the multi-layer perceptron. For this example, we will have two sets of hidden layers of 100 layers of neurons each, with a Softmax activation function, one of the most common functions used in data classification problems in neural networks.

Also, it is important to establish the number of inputs that the network will have, its total number of outputs, the size of each hidden layer, the name of each layer, or the size of each batch of examples to train, among others.

model:

```
!obj:pylearn2.models.mlp
.MLP { batch_size: 1,
nvis: 9,
layers: [ !obj:pylearn2.models.mlp.RectifiedLinear
        { layer_name: 'capa1',
        dim: 100,
        irange: .05,
        use_bias: true,
        max_col_norm:
        1.9365,
},
    !obj:pylearn2.models.mlp.RectifiedLinear
        { layer_name: 'capa2',
        dim: 100,
        irange: .05,
        use_bias: true,
        max_col_norm:
        1.9365,
```

```
                              },

                   !obj:pylearn2.models.mlp.Soft

                        max { max_col_norm:

                        1.9365, layer_name:

                        'output', n_classes: 1310,

                        istdev: .5

            }

            ],

            },
```

Finally, with our network almost completely built, we need to tell you what kind of training algorithm we are going to do. In particular, there are two major algorithms used in this type of artificial neural networks: the SGD (Stochastic Gradient Descent), which will be used in this network, and the BGD (Mini-Batch Gradient Descent).

These algorithms update the network parameter set iteratively to minimize an error function. While in the BGD, it is necessary to go through all the samples of the training set to make a single update of a parameter in a particular iteration, in the SGD, a single sample of its training set is used to make the update of a parameter in a particular iteration. This makes the DMS computationally faster and works better with large datasets.

In this section, important parameters will be specified, such as the learning rate, the monitoring variables that will give us information about each iteration of the network, or the number of times or iterations that will be carried out in training.

algorithm:

```
!obj:pylearn2.training_algorithms.sgd.SGD

{ batch_size: 1,

learning_rate: .001,

monitoring_dataset: {

        train : *train

},

termination_criterion: !obj:pylearn2.termination_criteria.And
{ criteria: [

        !obj:pylearn2.termination_criteria.EpochCounter

        { max_epochs: 100

        },

    ]

},

},
```

In addition to these three main features, it is possible to include numerous more additions to these training files, such as the monitoring of the better result of network training, storage of training results in an external file for later visualization or parameterization of features related to cost functions.

Training Results

To execute the training of the network, place the training file (train.py), which will be common to all networks, along with the YAML file built earlier and run the Python file passing as parameter our YAML file. If there has not been any syntax or execution error, our network will train the number of times we have requested in the YAML, showing in each iteration the value taken by the different monitoring variables.

Several options can be considered to interpret the results of artificial neural network training. Pylearn2 provides us with up to three scripts that allow us to know the final state of the training:

1. plot_monitor.py: This file allows us to generate a series of graphs referring to the monitoring variables used in network training.

2. print_monitor.py: In this file we can find the final value of the monitoring variables once the training is finished, as well as additional data such as the number of times trained, the total time of the training, the learning rate applied or the time taken in the last time.

    epochsseen: 100

    timetrained: 583.190377951

    learning_rate : 0.001

    total_seconds_last_epoch : 5.473321

train_capa1_col_norms_max : 1.9365

train_capa1_col_norms_mean : 1.37206941632

train_capa1_col_norms_min : 0.0660263708571

train_capa1_row_norms_max : 14.2793500939

train_capa1_row_norms_mean : 2.47378517442

train_capa1_row_norms_min : 0.151065377383

train_capa2_col_norms_max : 1.9365

train_capa2_col_norms_mean : 1.89316653221

train_capa2_col_norms_min : 0.303996630509

train_layer2_max_x_max_u : 0.630642358344

train_capa2_max_x_mean_u : 0.0360200089199

train_layer2_max_x_min_u : 0.0

train_capa2_mean_x_max_u : 0.630642358344

train_capa2_mean_x_mean_u : 0.0360200089199

train_capa2_mean_x_min_u : 0.0

train_layer2_min_x_max_u : 0.630642358344

train_capa2_min_x_mean_u : 0.0360200089199

train_layer2_min_x_min_u : 0.0

train_capa2_range_x_max_u : 0.0

train_capa2_range_x_mean_u : 0.0

train_capa2_range_x_min_u : 0.0

train_capa2_row_norms_max : 8.64138485606

train_capa2_row_norms_mean : 1.23119182706

train_capa2_row_norms_min : 0.0625394282101

train_objective : 7.04516868857

train_output_col_norms_max : 1.9365

train_output_col_norms_mean : 1.93537597233

train_output_col_norms_min : 1.82989682816

train_output_max_max_class : 0.00160358296479

train_output_mean_max_class : 0.00160358296479

train_exit_min_max_class : 0.00160358296479

train_output_misclass : 0.997607655502

train_output_nll : 7.04516868857

train_output_row_norms_max : 7.27668694755

train_output_row_norms_mean : 7.00343971194

train_output_row_norms_min : 6.60771031808

training_seconds_this_epoch : 2.777684

3. summarize_model.py: This third file shows us information about the number of examples and batches trained, the value of the weights and biases of the different layers of our model.

> layer1_W:(-1.9364999999402577,-0.15667975960821962, 0.055383367325278814)(9, 100) abs(layer1_W):(5.2213172409292608e-08,0.16558451646960629, 1.9364999999402577)
>
> capa1_W row norms:(0.15106537738270107, 2.4737851744236203, 14.279350093859149)
>
> capa1_W col norms:(0.066026370857087777, 1.3720694163217337, 1.9365000000000003)
>
> layer1_b: (-0.0037342685469777923, -0.00034371581074628074,
>
> 0.00079580419492335296)(100,)
>
> abs(capa1_b): (0.0, 0.0003673022839535406, 0.0037342685469777923)
>
> layer2_W: (-1.804490151648847, -0.054155046120049476,
>
> 1.8614267126998498)(100, 100)
>
> abs(capa2_W): (3.363048785339789e-09, 0.072040728728714409266,
>
> 1.8614267126998498)
>
> capa2_W row norms:(0.06253942821006922, 1.2311918270648283, 8.6413848560617907)

capa2_W col norms:(0.30399663050895098, 1.8931665322149838, 1.9365000000000006)

layer2_b: (-0.010058148991971261, 0.034804458245025476,

0.63064235834396398)(100,)

abs(capa2_b): (1.7200868128147963e-05, 0.037235559594865054,

0.63064235834396398)

softmax_b: (-0.04401879110525192, 1.1812010233368793e-18,

0.074194946099136613)(1310,)

abs(softmax_b): (0.021949618678901467, 0.042002948038271516,

0.074194946099136613)

softmax_W: (-1.0665771333338185, -1.9247737420458122e-05,

1.3741943065569819)(100, 1310)

abs(softmax_W): (7.2585513628129128e-07, 0.15411537138433551,

1.3741943065569819)

softmax_W row norms:(6.6077103180784729, 7.0034397119379772, 7.2766869475525171) softmax_W col norms:(1.829896828156788, 1.9353759723337318, 1.9365000000000008)

trained on 41800 examples

which corresponds to 41800 batches Trained for 0.161997327209 hours

100 epochs Training succeeded

4. show_weights.py: In case of having images as entrances of our network -instead of text files like this case- this script generates us an image of the weights once finished the training.

Artificial Neural Networks Case Studies

Having a set of data that are trained without problems using Pylearn2 and having at our disposal a large number of models of neural networks and different training algorithms provided by the library itself, we can study and investigate which parameters and characteristics work best for our data set.

In the study carried out, a total of 50 tests or training were carried out with six different models of artificial neural networks and the two training algorithms already mentioned above, and we observed the results of the training time-varying different parameters of the networks built.

It is important to note the great role played in Pylearn2 - and internally with Theano- by the GPU to improve performance in training networks. It is possible to perform very complex calculations at levels of this GPU, which in some cases allows showing substantially better results than in the same CPU, thus benefiting the results of the training. Performance over time will vary depending on the devices.

The network models used for this study are Multilayer Perceptrons (MLP) with three different activation functions (Gaussian, Sigmoid, and SoftMax), Boltzmann's Restricted Machine (RBM), Boltzmann's Deep Machine (DBM) and Autoencoders.

Model - Time

Models	Time
MLP - Softmax	8.52 minutes
MLP - Gaussian	8.29 minutes
MLP - Sigmoid	11.02 minutes
RBM	1.38 minutes
DBM	7.56 minutes
Autoencoders	0.3 minutes

Once the 50 pieces of training with 60 different nets have been carried out, the training time has been calculated for different models of neural nets that had 100 epochs, 100 hidden layers, and a learning index of 0.001 with the SGD algorithm, discovering the times described above.

The Multilayer Perceptrons are the models that perhaps would be less convenient at the level of training time, but they are one of the most stable models existing today because they can act as universal approximators of functions between a group of input and output variables, resulting in flexible tools and general purpose.

Boltzmann's machines, in theory, are much faster, especially the restricted one, although the more complex the problem is in practice, presents worse results. Something similar happens with Autoencoders that, although they have extremely short execution times, are more expensive, the more complex the problem is, with the addition of not being as flexible and stable as an MLP.

Model – Algorithm

Model	Algorithms (Medium)	
	DMS	BGD
MLP - Softmax	14.33 minutes	55.47 minutes
MLP - Gaussian	28.84 minutes	45.88 minutes
MLP - Sigmoid	16.57 minutes	72.54 minutes
RBM	3.27 minutes	5.08 minutes
DBM	14.35 minutes	1.73 minutes
Autoencoders	0.98 minutes	3.22 minutes

We can also glimpse noticeable differences if we compare the execution time of the training according to the algorithm used. The DMS is the algorithm that works best when we have variably large data sets rather than requiring a batch of samples, as is the case with BGD, which generally produces a greater computational effort that is reflected in time.

Model - Algorithm - Number of Layers

Models		Number of Layers (Average)	
		DMS	BGD
MLP - Softmax	50 layers	6.33 minutes	37.8 minutes
	100 layers	18.32 minutes	73.15 minutes
MLP - Gaussian	50 layers	6.48 minutes	14.29 minutes
	100 layers	50.6 minutes	61.67 minutes
MLP - Sigmoid	50 layers	5.63 minutes	70.09 minutes
	100 layers	22.04 minutes	74.99 minutes
RBM	100 layers	4.19 minutes	6 minutes
	200 layers	1.9 minutes	3.23 minutes
DBM	100 layers	16.11 minutes	2.06 minutes
	200 layers	11.72 minutes	1.08 minutes
Autoencoders	100 layers	1.2 minutes	3.54 minutes
	200 layers	0.56 minutes	2.6 minutes

The number of hidden layers in the model is also a factor to take into account when training a network, something that is also reflected in the training algorithm used. The MLP models have used hidden layers of 50 and 100 layers, showing that the greater the number of layers, the time used for training is significantly greater, as well as maintaining the same differences previously existing with the two algorithms used. It occurs oppositely in Boltzmann models and Autoencoders, where placing a greater number of layers reduces the execution time.

Model - Number of Layers - Learning Rate

Models		Learning Rate	
		0.001	0.1
MLP - Softmax	50 layers	6.36 minutes	6.31 minutes
	100 layers	21.1 minutes	9.99 minutes
MLP - Gaussian	50 layers	6.48 minutes	6.21 minutes
	100 layers	40.41 minutes	71 minutes
MLP - Sigmoid	50 layers	7.07 minutes	4.19 minutes
	100 layers	25.75 minutes	10.94 minutes
RBM	100 layers	5.53 minutes	1.52 minutes
	200 layers	1.81 minutes	2 minutes
DBM	100 layers	20.52 minutes	7.28 minutes
	200 layers	11.49 minutes	11.95 minutes
Autoencoders	100 layers	1.69 minutes	0.22 minutes
	200 layers	0.32 minutes	0.8 minutes

Less palpable is the study carried out taking into account the changes in the learning index, where -generically- it can be affirmed that the training execution time is reduced when the number of hidden layers of the network architecture and the learning rate itself increases.

Chapter Four

MULTILAYER PERCEPTRON

Getting Started with Multilayer Perceptrons

Neural networks are amazing, but they are painful to learn at first, involving a lot of terms and algorithms. This chapter mainly introduces the terminology and usage of a multi-layer perceptron. This chapter will:

- Introducing neurons, weights, and activation functions of neural networks

- How to build a network using building blocks

- How to train the network

let us start.

This section has a lot of content:

- Multilayer perceptron

- Neurons, weights, and activation functions

- Neural network

- Network training

Let's start with multilayer perceptrons.

Multilayer Perceptron

(Translator's Note: "Neural Network" in this book generally refers to "Artificial Neural Network")

In a general context, artificial neural networks generally refer to or Neural network, multilayer perceptron. Perceptrons are simple neuron models, precursors of large neural networks. This field focuses on how the brain solves complex computational problems through simple biological structures, such as making predictions. The ultimate goal is not to build a true model of the brain, but to discover algorithms that can solve complex problems.

The power of neural networks comes from the fact that it can learn from input data and predict the future: in this sense, neural networks learn a correspondence. Mathematically speaking, this ability is a universal approximation algorithm. The predictive power of neural networks comes from the hierarchical or multilayer structure of the network: this structure can find different features at different scales or resolutions and combine them into higher-level features, for example, from lines to collections of lines to shapes.

Neurons

A neural network consists of artificial neurons: these neurons have computational power, use activation functions, use inputs and weights, and output a scalar.

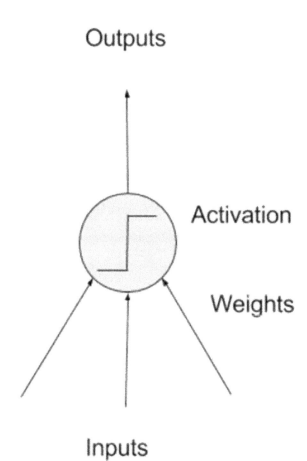

Neuron Weights

The weight of linear regression is similar to the weight here: each neuron also has an error term, which is always 1.0 and must be weighted. For example, if a neuron has two input values, then it needs three weight terms: one weight per input, plus the weight of an error term.

The initial value of the weight term is generally a small random number, for example, 0 ~ 0.3; there are also more complicated initialization methods. As with linear regression, the larger the weight, the more complex and unstable the network is. We want to make the weights smaller, and we can use regularization for this.

Activation Function

All neuron inputs are weighted and summed into the activation function. The activation function is the mapping of the weighted sum of inputs to the signal output. The activation function is named after its function: controlling which neuron is activated, and the output signal strength. The activation function in history is a threshold: for example, if the weighted input sum exceeds 0.5, it outputs 1; otherwise, it outputs 0.0.

The activation function generally uses a non-linear function so that the input combination can be more complicated and provide more functions. Non-linear functions can output a distribution: For example, a logical function (also known as an S-shaped function) outputs an S-shaped distribution between 0 and 1, and a tangent function can output an S-shaped distribution between -1 and 1. Recent studies have shown that linear rectification functions work better.

Neural Networks

Neurons can form a network: each row of neurons is called a layer, and a neural network can have many layers. The structure of a neural network is called network topology.

Input Layer

The bottom layer of the neural network is called the input layer because it is directly connected to the data. The general number of nodes is the number of columns of data. Neurons in this layer only transfer data to the next layer.

Hidden Layers

The layer behind the input node is called the hidden layer because it is not directly connected to the outside world. In the simplest network, there is only one neuron in the hidden layer, which directly outputs the result. With the increase in computing power, it is now possible to train very complexly, high-layer neural networks: networks that historically required several lifetimes to train can now be trained in minutes.

Output Layer

The last layer of the neural network is called the output layer, which outputs the values needed for the problem. The activation function at this level depends on the type of problem:

- Simple regression problem: it is possible to have only one neuron and no activation function

- The classification of two items: there may be only one neuron, the activation function is an S-type function, and a probability between 0 and 1 is output, which represents the probability of the main category. You can also use 0.5 as the threshold: less than 0.5 outputs 0, and greater than 0.5 outputs 1.

- Multi-class classification problem: It is possible to have multiple neurons, each representing a class (for example, three neurons, representing three different irises-this is a classic problem). The activation function can use the Softmax function, and each output represents the probability of being a certain category. The most likely category is the one with the highest output.

Network Training

Preliminary Data

Preprocess the data: the data must be numeric, for example, real. If an item is a category, it needs to be turned into a number by one-hot encoding: for N possible categories, add N columns, and take 0 or 1 to represent whether it belongs to the category.

One-hot encoding can also encode multiple categories: build a binary vector to represent the categories, and the output can be used to classify the categories. Neural networks require all data units to be similar: for example, scaling all data to between 0 and 1 is called normalization. Alternatively, scale (regularize) the data so that the average of each column is 0 and the standard deviation is 1. The pixel data of the image should also be processed this way. Text input can be converted into numbers, such as how often a word appears, or by other methods.

Stochastic Gradient Descent

Stochastic gradient descent is classic and still popular today. The method used is forward transfer: input one line of data to the network at a time, activate each layer of neurons, and get an output value. Predict the data this way.

We compare the output with the expected value to calculate the error; this error propagates back through the network and updates the weight data. This algorithm is called the backpropagation algorithm. We repeat this process on all the training data, and each time the network is updated is called a round. Neural networks can train dozens or even thousands of rounds.

Weight Update

The weight of the neural network can be updated every time it is trained. This method is called the online update, which is fast but may cause catastrophic results. Or you can save the error data and update it only once: this kind of update is called batch update, which is generally more secure.

Because the data set may be large, to calculate the speed, the amount of data updated each time is generally not large, only tens to hundreds of data. The number of weight updates is controlled by the learning rate (step size) parameter, which specifies how fast the neural network can respond to errors. This parameter is generally small, 0.1 or 0.01, or even smaller. You can also adjust other parameters:

- Momentum: If the direction is the same as last time, accelerate the change, even if the error is not so great this time. Used to speed up network training.

- Learning rate decay: The learning rate decreases as the number of training increases. Speed up training at the beginning and fine-tune the parameters later.

Making Predictions

The trained neural network can make predictions. You can use test data to measure and see if you can predict new data; you can also deploy a network to make predictions. The network only needs to save the topology and final weights. Feed the new data, and after the forward transmission, the neural network will make predictions.

This section was about machine learning with artificial neural networks.

- Neural networks are not models of the brain, but computational models that can solve complex machine learning problems

- A neural network consists of neurons with weights and activation functions

- Neural network layering, training with stochastic gradient descent

- Data should be preprocessed

You've learned about neural networks: In the next section, we will make our first neural network with Keras.

Developing Neural Networks with Keras

Keras is based on Python, and it is easy to develop deep learning models. Keras encapsulates the numerical calculations of Theano and TensorFlow and can configure and train neural networks in a few words. This chapter begins developing neural networks using Keras. This chapter will:

- Read CSV data into Keras

- Configure and compile a multilayer perceptron model with Keras

- Validate Keras model with the validation dataset

let us start.

Although the amount of code is small, let's take it slowly. There are several steps:

- Import Data

- Defining the model

- Compile model

- Training model

- Test model

- Write the program

Pima Diabetes Dataset

We use the Pima Indians onset of diabetes, which can be downloaded for free from UCI's machine learning website. The dataset contains medical records of Pima people and whether they have had diabetes in the past five years. All data are numbers, the question is (whether there is diabetes is 1 or 0), it is a binary classification problem. The magnitude of the data is different, with eight attributes:

1. Number of pregnancy

2. Plasma glucose concentration in a 2-hour oral glucose tolerance test

3. Diastolic blood pressure (mmHg)

4. 2 hours of serum insulin (mu U / ml)

5. Body mass index (BMI)

6. Diabetic bloodline function

7. Age (year)

8. Category: Whether you have diabetes in the past five years

All data is digital and can be imported directly into Keras. This data set will also be used later in this book. The data has 768 rows, and the sample of the first five rows looks like this:

6,148,72,35,0,33.6,0.627,50,1

1,85,66,29,0,26.6,0.351,31,0

8,183,64,0,0,23.3,0.672,32,1

1,89,66,23,94,28.1,0.167,21,0

0,137,40,35,168,43.1,2.288,33,1

The data is in the data directory of the book's code and can also be downloaded from the UCI Machine Learning website. Put the data with the Python file and rename it:

pima-indians-diabetes.csv

The benchmark accuracy rate is 65.1%, and the highest accuracy rate in 77 cross-validations is 77.7%. More information on the dataset can be found on the UCI machine learning website.

Import Data

When using stochastic gradient descent, it is best to fix the random number seed so that your code will run consistently every time. This is especially effective when demonstrating results, comparing algorithms, or debugging. You can choose your seeds:

```
# fix random seed for reproducibility

seed = 7

numpy.random.seed(seed)
```

Now import the Pima dataset. NumPy's loadtxt()function can directly bring in data, with eight input variables and one output. After importing the data, we split the data into input and output groups for cross-checking:

load pima indians dataset

dataset   =   numpy.loadtxt("pima-indians-diabetes.csv", delimiter=",")

split into input (X) and output (Y) variables

X = dataset[:,0:8]

Y – dataset[:,8]

In this way, our data is consistent every time, and the model can be defined.

Defining the Model

Keras' model consists of layers: we build a Sequential model and add neurons layer by layer. The first step is to make sure that the number of input layers is correct: input_dimdetermine it with parameters when creating the model. For example, if there are eight input variables, set it to 8.

How to set the hidden layer? This question is difficult to answer and needs to be tested slowly. In general, if the network is large enough, it won't matter even if there are problems. In this example, we use a 3-layer fully-connected network.

The fully connected layer is Densedefined by a class: the first parameter is the number of neurons in this layer, then the initialization method and activation function. The initialization method here is a continuous uniform distribution of 0 to 0.05 (uniform), as is the default method of Keras. It can also be initialized with a Gaussian distribution (normal).

The activation function of the first two layers is a linear rectification function (relu), and the activation function of the last layer is an S-type function (sigmoid). Before, everyone liked to use S-type and tangent functions, but now linear rectification functions work better. To ensure that the output is a probability number from 0 to 1, the activation function of the last layer is an S-type function, so that it is easy to map to a threshold function of 0.5. The first two hidden layers have 12 and 8 neurons, respectively, and the last layer is one neuron (whether or not there is diabetes).

```
# create model

model = Sequential ()

model.add (Dense (12, input_dim = 8, init = 'uniform',
activation = 'relu')) model.add (Dense (8, init = 'uniform',
activation = 'relu')) model.add ( Dense (1, init = 'uniform',
activation = 'sigmoid'))
```

The structure of the network is shown in the figure:

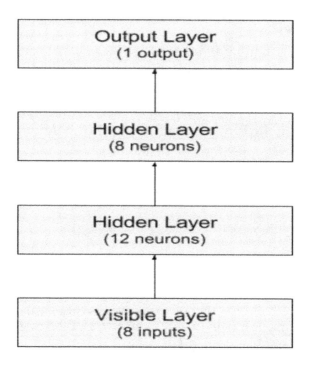

Compile Model

The defined model can be compiled: Keras will call Theano or TensorFlow to compile the model. The backend will automatically choose the best way to represent the network with your hardware. This step requires the definition of several new parameters. The significance of training a neural network is to find the best set of weights and solve the problem.

We need to define loss functions and optimization algorithms and the data we need to collect. We use the binary_crossentropywrong logarithm as a loss function; Adamas an optimization algorithm because this thing works well. For more information, please read Adam: A Method for Stochastic Optimization. Because this problem is a classification problem, we collect the accuracy of each round.

Training Model

Finally, start training! Call the model's fit()method to start training.

The network is trained in rounds and nb_epochcontrolled by parameters. The data (batch size) fed in each time can be batch_sizecontrolled by parameters. Here we only run 150 rounds with 10 data each time. Just try it out.

```
# Fit the model
model.fit(X, Y, nb_epoch=150, batch_size=10)
```

Now the CPU or GPU starts frying eggs.

Test Model

Let's take out the test data to check the effect of the model. Note that this does not test the predictive power of new data. The data should be split into training and test sets.

Call the evaluation()method of the model and pass in the training data. The output is the average, including the average error and other data, such as accuracy.

```
# evaluate the model
scores = model.evaluate(X, Y)
print("%s: %.2f%%" % (model.metrics_names[1],
scores[1]*100))
```

Write the Program

Machine learning with Keras is as simple as that. We put the code together:

```
# Create first network with Keras
```

```python
from keras.models import Sequential

from keras.layers import Dense

import numpy

# fix random seed for reproducibility

seed = 7

numpy.random.seed (seed)

# load pima indians dataset

dataset = numpy.loadtxt ("pima-indians-diabetes.csv",
delimiter = ",")

# split into input (X) and output (Y) variables

X = dataset [:, 0: 8]

Y = dataset [:, 8]

# create model

model = Sequential ()

model.add (Dense (12, input_dim = 8, init = 'uniform',
activation = 'relu')) model.add (Dense (8, init = 'uniform',
activation = 'relu'))

model.add (Dense (1, init = 'uniform', activation = 'sigmoid'))

# Compile model

model.compile (loss = 'binary_crossentropy', optimizer =
'adam', metrics = ['accuracy']) # Fit the model
```

```
model.fit (X, Y, nb_epoch = 150, batch_size = 10)

# evaluate the model

scores = model.evaluate (X, Y)

print ("% s:% .2f %%"% (model.metrics_names [1], scores
[1] * 100))
```

During training, each round will output loss and accuracy, and the final effect. Run Theano on my CPU for about 10 seconds:

```
Epoch 143/150

768/768 [==============================] - 0s -
loss: 0.4614 - acc: 0.7878

Epoch 144/150

768/768 [==============================] - 0s -
loss: 0.4508 - acc: 0.7969

Epoch 145/150

768/768 [==============================] - 0s -
loss: 0.4580 - acc: 0.7747

Epoch 146/150

768/768 [==============================] - 0s -
loss: 0.4627 - acc: 0.7812

Epoch 147/150

768/768 [==============================] - 0s -
loss: 0.4531 - acc: 0.7943
```

Epoch 148/150

768/768 [==============================] - 0s - loss: 0.4656 - acc: 0.7734

Epoch 149/150

768/768 [==============================] - 0s - loss: 0.4566 - acc: 0.7839

Epoch 150/150

768/768 [==============================] - 0s - loss: 0.4593 - acc: 0.7839

768/768 [==============================] - 0s

acc: 79.56%

This section was about creating neural networks with Keras. in conclusion:

- How to import data

- How to define a neural network with Keras

- How to call the backend compilation model

- How to train the model

- How to test the model

Now you know how to develop neural networks with Keras: the next section tells how to test on new data.

Testing Neural Networks

There are many parameters to adjust in deep learning: most of them are headshots. So testing is particularly important: in this section, we discuss several testing methods. This chapter will:

- Automatic verification with Keras

- Manual verification with Keras

- K-fold cross-validation with Keras

let us start.

Oral Neural Networks

There are many parameters when creating a neural network: Many times, it can be copied from other people's networks, but in the end, it still takes a little experimentation. Whether it is the network topology (number of layers, size, type of each layer) or small parameters (loss function, activation function, optimization algorithm, training times), etc.

In general, deep learning datasets are large, with hundreds of thousands or even hundreds of millions of data. So test methods are crucial.

Dividing Data

A large amount of data and the complex network will cause a long training time, so the data needs to be divided into training, testing, or validation data sets. Keras offers two approaches:

1. Automatic verification

2. Manual verification

Automatic Verification

Keras can automatically divide the data into a part and verify it after each training. During training, validation_splityou can use parameters to specify the proportion of validation data, which is generally 20% or 33% of the total data. The following code adds automatic verification to previous section (Developing Neural Networks:

```
# MLP with automatic validation set

from keras.models import Sequential

from keras.layers import Dense

import numpy

# fix random seed for reproducibility

seed = 7

numpy.random.seed (seed)

# load pima indians dataset

dataset = numpy.loadtxt ("pima-indians-diabetes.csv",
delimiter = ",")

# split into input (X) and output (Y) variables

X = dataset [:, 0: 8]

Y = dataset [:, 8]

# create model

model = Sequential ()
```

```
model.add (Dense (12, input_dim = 8, init = 'uniform',
activation = 'relu')) model.add (Dense (8, init = 'uniform',
activation = 'relu'))

model.add (Dense (1, init = 'uniform', activation = 'sigmoid'))

# Compile model

model.compile (loss = 'binary_crossentropy', optimizer =
'adam', metrics = ['accuracy']) # Fit the model

model.fit (X, Y, validation_split = 0.33, nb_epoch = 150,
batch_size = 10)
```

During training, data for training and test data is displayed
for each round:

Epoch 145/150

514/514 [==============================] - 0s -
loss: 0.4885 - acc: 0.7743 - val_loss:

   0.5016 - val_acc: 0.7638

Epoch 146/150

514/514 [==============================] - 0s -
loss: 0.4862 - acc: 0.7704 - val_loss:

   0.5202 - val_acc: 0.7323

Epoch 147/150

514/514 [==============================] - 0s -
loss: 0.4959 - acc: 0.7588 - val_loss:

0.5012 - val_acc: 0.7598

Epoch 148/150

514/514 [==============================] - 0s - loss: 0.4966 - acc: 0.7665 - val_loss:

   0.5244 - val_acc: 0.7520

Epoch 149/150

514/514 [==============================] - 0s - loss: 0.4863 - acc: 0.7724 - val_loss:

   0.5074 - val_acc: 0.7717

Epoch 150/150

514/514 [==============================] - 0s - loss: 0.4884 - acc: 0.7724 - val_loss:

   0.5462 - val_acc: 0.7205

Manual Verification

Keras can also be verified manually. We define a train_test_splitfunction that divides the data into a 2: 1 test and validation data set. When calling the fit()method, you need to add validation_dataparameters as validation data. The items of the array are input and output data, respectively.

```
# MLP with manual validation set

from keras.models import Sequential

from keras.layers import Dense
```

```python
from sklearn.cross_validation import train_test_split

import numpy

# fix random seed for reproducibility

seed = 7

numpy.random.seed (seed)

# load pima indians dataset

dataset = numpy.loadtxt ("pima-indians-diabetes.csv",
delimiter = ",")

# split into input (X) and output (Y) variables

X = dataset [:, 0: 8]

Y = dataset [:, 8]

# split into 67% for train and 33% for test

X_train, X_test, y_train, y_test = train_test_split (X, Y,
test_size = 0.33, random_state = seed) # create model

model = Sequential ()

model.add (Dense (12, input_dim = 8, init = 'uniform',
activation = 'relu'))

model.add (Dense (8, init = 'uniform', activation = 'relu'))

model.add (Dense (1, init = 'uniform', activation = 'sigmoid'))

# Compile model
```

model.compile (loss = 'binary_crossentropy', optimizer = 'adam', metrics = ['accuracy'])

Fit the model

model.fit (X_train, y_train, validation_data = (X_test, y_test), nb_epoch = 150, batch_size = 10)

As with automated verification, Keras will output training and verification results after each training round:

Epoch 145/150

514/514 [==============================] - 0s - loss: 0.5001 - acc: 0.7685 - val_loss:

  0.5617 - val_acc: 0.7087

Epoch 146/150

514/514 [==============================] - 0s - loss: 0.5041 - acc: 0.7529 - val_loss:

  0.5423 - val_acc: 0.7362

Epoch 147/150

514/514 [==============================] - 0s - loss: 0.4936 - acc: 0.7685 - val_loss:

  0.5426 - val_acc: 0.7283

Epoch 148/150

514/514 [==============================] - 0s - loss: 0.4957 - acc: 0.7685 - val_loss:

0.5430 - val_acc: 0.7362

Epoch 149/150

514/514 [==============================] - 0s - loss: 0.4953 - acc: 0.7685 - val_loss:

0.5403 - val_acc: 0.7323

Epoch 150/150

514/514 [==============================] - 0s - loss: 0.4941 - acc: 0.7743 - val_loss:

0.5452 - val_acc: 0.7323

Manual K-fold Cross-Validation

The golden rule of machine learning is K-fold verification to verify the model's ability to predict future data. The K-fold verification method is: divide the data into K groups, leaving 1 group for verification and other data for training until the performance of each distribution is consistent.

Deep learning generally does not require cross-validation because the computing power is too high. For example, the number of K-folds is generally 50 or 10 fold: each group needs to be trained and verified, and the training time is multiplied. However, if the amount of data is small, the effect of cross-validation is better and the error is smaller.

scikit-learn has StratifiedKFoldclasses, we use it to divide the data into 10 groups. The sampling method is stratified sampling to ensure that the amount of data in each group is consistent. Then we train the model on each group, using verbose=0parameters to turn off the output of each round. After training, Keras will output the performance of the model and store the model. In the end, the average and standard deviation of Keras output performance provides a more accurate estimate for performance estimation:

```
# MLP for Pima Indians Dataset with 10-fold cross validation

from keras.models import Sequential

from keras.layers import Dense

from sklearn.cross_validation import StratifiedKFold

import numpy

# fix random seed for reproducibility

seed = 7

numpy.random.seed(seed)

# load pima indians dataset

dataset    =    numpy.loadtxt("pima-indians-diabetes.csv",
delimiter=",")

# split into input (X) and output (Y) variables

X = dataset[:,0:8]

Y = dataset[:,8]

# define 10-fold cross validation test harness

kfold  =  StratifiedKFold(y=Y, n_folds=10, shuffle=True,
random_state=seed)

cvscores = []
```

```
for i, (train, test) in enumerate(kfold):

    # create model

    model = Sequential()

    model.add(Dense(12, input_dim=8, init='uniform',
    activation='relu')) model.add(Dense(8, init='uniform',
    activation='relu'))

    model.add(Dense(1,                        init='uniform',
    activation='sigmoid'))

    # Compile model

    model.compile(loss='binary_crossentropy',
    optimizer='adam', metrics=['accuracy']) # Fit the
    model

model.fit(X[train], Y[train], nb_epoch=150, batch_size=10,
verbose=0)

    # evaluate the model

    scores = model.evaluate(X[test], Y[test], verbose=0)

    print("%s: %.2f%%" % (model.metrics_names[1],
    scores[1]*100)) cvscores.append(scores[1] * 100)

    print("%.2f%%        (+/-        %.2f%%)"        %
    (numpy.mean(cvscores), numpy.std(cvscores)))
```

The output is:

acc: 77.92%

acc: 79.22%

acc: 76.62%

acc: 77.92%

acc: 75.32%

acc: 74.03%

acc: 77.92%

acc: 71.43%

acc: 71.05%

acc: 75.00%

75.64% (+/- 2.67%)

Each cycle needs to regenerate the model and train with the corresponding data. In the next chapter we use scikit-learn to directly use Keras' model.

In this section, we discussed about testing the performance of neural networks. In conclusion:

- How to automatically split data into training and test groups

- How to manually group data

- How to test performance using K-fold

Now that you know how to test the performance of neural networks: the next section tells how to use Keras models directly in Scikit-learn.

Calling Keras' Model Using Scikit-Learn

Scikit-learn is the most popular Python machine learning library. In this section, we will use Scikit-learn to call the model generated by Keras. This chapter will:

- Modeling Keras with Scikit-learn

- Cross-validation of Keras' model using Scikit-learn

- Use Scikit-learn to adjust the hyperparameters of the Keras model using grid search

let us start.

Keras is popular in deep learning, but it can only do deep learning: Keras is a minimized deep learning library, and the goal is to build deep learning models quickly. Based on SciPy's Scikit-learn, the numerical operation is very efficient, suitable for general machine learning tasks, and provides many machine learning tools, including but not limited to:

- K-fold validation model

- Quickly search and test hyperparameters

Keras encapsulates KerasClassifierand for Scikit-learn KerasRegressor. In this chapter, we continue to use the model from Chapter 7.

Testing Cross-Validation Deep Learning Models

Keras KerasClassifierand KerasRegressortwo classes accept build_fnparameters and pass in the compiled model. Join us nb_epoch=150and batch_size=10these two parameters: These two parameters will be passed in the model fit()methods. We use scikit-learn's StratifiedKFoldclass to perform 10-fold cross-validation, test the model's performance on unknown data, and use cross_val_score()functions to detect the model and print the results.

```
# MLP for Pima Indians Dataset with 10-fold cross validation
via sklearn

from keras.models import Sequential

from keras.layers import Dense

from keras.wrappers.scikit_learn import KerasClassifier

from sklearn.cross_validation import StratifiedKFold

from sklearn.cross_validation import cross_val_score

import numpy

import pandas

# Function to create model, required for KerasClassifier

def create_model():

    # create model

    model = Sequential()

    model.add(Dense(12, input_dim=8, init='uniform',
activation='relu'))    model.add(Dense(8,    init='uniform',
activation='relu'))    model.add(Dense(1,    init='uniform',
activation='sigmoid'))

    # Compile model
```

```
    model.compile(loss='binary_crossentropy',
    optimizer='adam', metrics=['accuracy']) return model
```

fix random seed for reproducibility

seed = 7

numpy.random.seed(seed)

load pima indians dataset

dataset = numpy.loadtxt("pima-indians-diabetes.csv", delimiter=",")

split into input (X) and output (Y) variables

X = dataset[:,0:8]

Y = dataset[:,8]

create model

model = KerasClassifier(build_fn=create_model, nb_epoch=150, batch_size=10)

evaluate using 10-fold cross validation

kfold = StratifiedKFold(y=Y, n_folds=10, shuffle=True, random_state=seed)

results = cross_val_score(model, X, Y, cv=kfold)

print(results.mean())

Each round of training will output a result, plus the final average performance:

Epoch 145/150

692/692 [==============================] - 0s -
loss: 0.4671 - acc: 0.7803

Epoch 146/150

692/692 [==============================] - 0s -
loss: 0.4661 - acc: 0.7847

Epoch 147/150

692/692 [==============================] - 0s -
loss: 0.4581 - acc: 0.7803

Epoch 148/150

692/692 [==============================] - 0s -
loss: 0.4657 - acc: 0.7688

Epoch 149/150

692/692 [==============================] - 0s -
loss: 0.4660 - acc: 0.7659

Epoch 150/150

692/692 [==============================] - 0s -
loss: 0.4574 - acc: 0.7702

76/76 [==============================] - 0s

0.756442244065

Using scikit-learn is much easier than manual testing.

Adjusting the Parameters of a Deep Learning Model using Grid Search

The model for wrapping Keras with Scikit-learn is very simple. Further thinking: We can fit()pass parameters to methods, KerasClassifierand build_fnmethods can also pass parameters. You can use this to adjust the model further.

We use a grid search to test the performance of different parameters: create_model()functions can be passed in the optimizer and init parameters, although both have default values. Then we can adjust the network with different optimization algorithms and initial weights. Specifically, we want to search:

- Optimization Algorithm: Method of Searching Weights

- Initial weight: Initialize different networks

- Training times: the number of times the model was trained

- Batch size: the amount of data per training

All the parameters form a dictionary and are passed to the Scikit-learn GridSearchCVclass: GridSearchCVeach group of parameters ($2 \times 3 \times 3 \times 3$) is trained and a 3-fold cross-check is performed.

The amount of calculation is huge: it takes a long time. If the model is small, you can also try to take part of the data. The model from Chapter 7 works because neither the network nor the data set is large (within 1000 data, 9 parameters). Finally scikit-learn will output the best parameters and models, as well as the average.

MLP for Pima Indians Dataset with grid search via sklearn

from keras.models import Sequential

```python
from keras.layers import Dense

from keras.wrappers.scikit_learn import KerasClassifier

from sklearn.grid_search import GridSearchCV

import numpy

import pandas

# Function to create model, required for KerasClassifier

def create_model(optimizer='rmsprop',
init='glorot_uniform'):

    # create model

    model = Sequential()

    model.add(Dense(12, input_dim=8, init=init,
activation='relu')) model.add(Dense(8, init=init,
activation='relu')) model.add(Dense(1, init=init,
activation='sigmoid'))

    # Compile model

    model.compile(loss='binary_crossentropy',
optimizer=optimizer, metrics=['accuracy']) return model

# fix random seed for reproducibility

seed = 7

numpy.random.seed(seed)

# load pima indians dataset
```

```
dataset = numpy.loadtxt("pima-indians-diabetes.csv",
delimiter=",")

# split into input (X) and output (Y) variables

X = dataset[:,0:8]

Y = dataset[:,8]

# create model

model = KerasClassifier(build_fn=create_model)

# grid search epochs, batch size and optimizer

optimizers = ['rmsprop', 'adam']

init = ['glorot_uniform', 'normal', 'uniform']

epochs = numpy.array([50, 100, 150])

batches = numpy.array([5, 10, 20])

param_grid = dict(optimizer=optimizers, nb_epoch=epochs,
batch_size=batches, init=init) grid =
GridSearchCV(estimator=model, param_grid=param_grid)

grid_result = grid.fit(X, Y)

# summarize results

print("Best: %f using %s" % (grid_result.best_score_,
grid_result.best_params_))

for params, mean_score, scores in grid_result.grid_scores_:
```

```
print("%f (%f) with: %r" % (scores.mean(),
scores.std(), params))
```

It takes almost 5 minutes to use the CPU, and the result is as follows. We found that using a uniform distribution initialization and rmspropoptimization algorithm, 150 rounds, the batch size is 5, the best effect, the accuracy rate is about 75%:

Best: 0.751302 using {'init': 'uniform', 'optimizer': 'rmsprop', 'nb_epoch': 150, 'batch_size': 5}

0.653646 (0.031948) with: {'init': 'glorot_uniform', 'optimizer': 'rmsprop', 'nb_epoch': 50, 'batch_size': 5}

0.665365 (0.004872) with: {'init': 'glorot_uniform', 'optimizer': 'adam', 'nb_epoch': 50, 'batch_size': 5}

0.683594 (0.037603) with: {'init': 'glorot_uniform', 'optimizer': 'rmsprop', 'nb_epoch': 100, 'batch_size': 5}

0.709635 (0.034987) with: {'init': 'glorot_uniform', 'optimizer': 'adam', 'nb_epoch': 100, 'batch_size': 5}

0.699219 (0.009568) with: {'init': 'glorot_uniform', 'optimizer': 'rmsprop', 'nb_epoch': 150, 'batch_size': 5}

0.725260 (0.008027) with: {'init': 'glorot_uniform', 'optimizer': 'adam', 'nb_epoch': 150, 'batch_size': 5}

0.686198 (0.024774) with: {'init': 'normal', 'optimizer': 'rmsprop', 'nb_epoch': 50, 'batch_size': 5}

0.718750 (0.014616) with: {'init': 'normal', 'optimizer': 'adam', 'nb_epoch': 50, 'batch_size': 5}

0.725260 (0.028940) with: {'init': 'normal', 'optimizer': 'rmsprop', 'nb_epoch': 100, 'batch_size': 5}

0.727865 (0.028764) with: {'init': 'normal', 'optimizer': 'adam', 'nb_epoch': 100, 'batch_size': 5}

0.748698 (0.035849) with: {'init': 'normal', 'optimizer': 'rmsprop', 'nb_epoch': 150, 'batch_size': 5}

0.712240 (0.039623) with: {'init': 'normal', 'optimizer': 'adam', 'nb_epoch': 150, 'batch_size': 5}

0.699219 (0.024910) with: {'init': 'uniform', 'optimizer': 'rmsprop', 'nb_epoch': 50, 'batch_size': 5}

0.703125 (0.011500) with: {'init': 'uniform', 'optimizer': 'adam', 'nb_epoch': 50, 'batch_size': 5}

0.720052 (0.015073) with: {'init': 'uniform', 'optimizer': 'rmsprop', 'nb_epoch': 100, 'batch_size': 5}

0.712240 (0.034987) with: {'init': 'uniform', 'optimizer': 'adam', 'nb_epoch': 100, 'batch_size': 5}

0.751302 (0.031466) with: {'init': 'uniform', 'optimizer': 'rmsprop', 'nb_epoch': 150, 'batch_size': 5}

0.734375 (0.038273) with: {'init': 'uniform', 'optimizer': 'adam', 'nb_epoch': 150, 'batch_size': 5}

This section was about using Scikit-learn to encapsulate and test the performance of neural networks.

- How to use Keras model with Scikit-learn

- How to test the performance of Keras models using Scikit-learn

- How to adjust hyperparameters of Keras model using Scikit-learn

Using Scikit-learn to adjust parameters is much easier than manually invoking Keras.

Now you know how to call the Keras model in Scikit-learn: you can start working. In the next sections of this chapter, we will use Keras to create different end-to-end models, starting with multi-class classification problems.

Project: Multi-Class Flower Classification

In this section, we use Keras to develop and validate a neural network for multi-class classification. This chapter includes:

- Import CSV into Keras

- Preprocessing data for Keras

- Keras model validation using Scikit-learn

let us start.

Iris Classification Data Set

In this chapter, we use the classic iris dataset. This data set has been fully researched. The four input variables are all numbers, and the dimensions are all centimeters. Each data represents different parameters of the flower, and the output is the classification result. The attributes of the data are (cm):

1. Sepal length

2. Sepal width

3. Petal length

4. Petal width

5. Category

This problem is multi-class classification: there are more than two categories that need to be predicted, to be precise, three. This problem requires special adjustments to the neural network. There are 150 data: the first five rows are:

5.1,3.5,1.4,0.2,Iris-setosa

4.9,3.0,1.4,0.2,Iris-setosa

4.7,3.2,1.3,0.2,Iris-setosa

4.6,3.1,1.5,0.2,Iris-setosa

5.0,3.6,1.4,0.2,Iris-setosa

The iris data set has been fully studied, and the accuracy of the model can reach 95% to 97%, which is a good target. Sample data and data are attached to the data directory of this book, which can also be downloaded from the UCI machine learning website and renamed iris.csv. Details of the dataset are available on the UCI Machine Learning website.

Importing Libraries and Functions

We import the required libraries and functions, including the deep learning package Keras, the data processing package pandas, and the model test package Scikit-learn.

```
import numpy
```

```
import pandas

from keras.models import Sequential

from keras.layers import Dense

from keras.wrappers.scikit_learn import KerasClassifier

from keras.utils import np_utils

from sklearn.cross_validation import cross_val_score

from sklearn.cross_validation import KFold

from sklearn.preprocessing import LabelEncoder

from sklearn.pipeline import Pipeline
```

Specifying a Random Number Seed

We specify a random number seed so that the results of repeated runs will be consistent to reproduce the results of random gradient descent:

```
# fix random seed for reproducibility

seed = 7

numpy.random.seed(seed)
```

Importing Data

Data can be imported directly. Because the data contains characters, it is easier to use pandas. The attributes (columns) of the data can then be divided into input variables (X) and output variables (Y):

```
# load dataset

dataframe = pandas.read_csv("iris.csv", header=None)
```

```
dataset = dataframe.values

X = dataset[:,0:4].astype(float)

Y = dataset[:,4]
```

Output Variable Encoding

The type of data is a string: when using a neural network, the categories should be encoded into a matrix, and each row and column represents the category to which it belongs. You can use one-hot encoding or add a column. This data has three categories: Iris-setosa, Iris-versicolor, and Iris-virginica. If the data is

Iris-setosa

Iris-versicolor

Iris-virginica

One-hot encoding can be used to encode such a matrix:

Iris-setosa, Iris-versicolor, Iris-virginica 1, 0, 0

0, 1, 0

0, 0, 1

Scikit-learn LabelEncodercan turn categories into numbers and then to_categorical()encode them with Keras functions:

```
# encode class values as integers

encoder = LabelEncoder()

encoder.fit(Y)
```

encoded_Y = encoder.transform(Y)

convert integers to dummy variables (i.e., one-hot encoded)

dummy_y = np_utils.to_categorical(encoded_Y)

Designing Neural Networks

Keras provides KerasClassifier; you can encapsulate the network and use it on Scikit-learn. KerasClassifierThe initialization variable is the model name and returns the neural network model for training.

We write a function to create a neural network for the iris classification problem: this fully-connected network has only one hidden layer with 4 neurons, the same number of variables as input. For the effect, the hidden layer uses the rectification function as the activation function. Because we use one-hot coding, the output of the network must be 3 variables, each variable represents a flower, and the largest variable represents the type of prediction. The structure of the network is:

4 neurons input layer-> [4 neurons hidden layer]-> 3 neurons output layer

The function of the output layer is an sigmoid function that maps the likelihood to a probability of 0 to 1. The optimization algorithm selects ADAM stochastic gradient descent, and the loss function is a logarithmic function, which is called in Keras categorical_crossentropy:

define baseline model

def baseline_model():

create model

107

```
model = Sequential()

model.add(Dense(4, input_dim=4, init='normal',
activation='relu')) model.add(Dense(3, init='normal',
activation='sigmoid'))

# Compile model

model.compile(loss='categorical_crossentropy',
optimizer='adam', metrics=['accuracy']) return model
```

You can create it with this model KerasClassifier, or you can pass in other parameters, which will be passed to the fit()function. We set the training times nb_epochto 150, the batch size batch_sizeto 5, and verbose0 to turn off debugging information:

```
estimator = KerasClassifier(build_fn=baseline_model,
nb_epoch=200, batch_size=5, verbose=0)
```

Test Model with K-Fold Cross Test

Now you can test the effect of the model. Scikit-learn has many ways to test the model, the most important of which is the K-fold test. We first set the test method of the model: K is set to 10 (the default value is good), and the data is randomly rearranged before segmentation:

```
kfold = KFold(n=len(X), n_folds=10, shuffle=True,
random_state=seed)
```

In this way, we can use the 10-fold cross-check ( ) on the dataset (Xand dummy_y) to kfoldtest the performance. The model takes 10 seconds to run, and the output of each test:

```
results = cross_val_score(estimator, X, dummy_y, cv=kfold)
```

```
print("Accuracy: %.2f%% (%.2f%%)" %
(results.mean()*100, results.std()*100))
```

Output the mean and standard deviation of the results, which can verify the predictive ability of the model, and the effect is outstanding:

Baseline: 95.33% (4.27%)

This chapter was about developing deep learning projects with Keras.

- How to import data

- How to use multi-class classification data with one-hot encoding

- How to use Keras with Scikit-learn

- How to define a multi-class classification neural network with Keras

- How to test Keras' model with Scikit-learn through K-fold cross-check

In this project, we fully described the development of the Keras project: in the next project, we develop a binary classification network and tune it.

Project: Sonar Return Value Classification

In this section, we use Keras to develop a binary classification network. This project includes:

- Importing data into Keras

- Define and train models for tabular data

- Testing the performance of Keras models on unknown data

- Process data to improve accuracy

- Adjust the topology and configuration of the Keras model

let us start.

Sonar Object Classification Data

This chapter uses sonar data, including the return of sonar in different objects. The data has 60 variables, which represent the return values from different angles. The goal is to separate the stone from the metal tube (ore).

All data is continuous, from 0 to 1. In the output variables, M represents the ore, and R represents the stone, which needs to be converted to 1 and 0. The data set has 208 pieces of data. You can also download and rename it in the data directory of this book, sonar.csv.

This data set can be used as a performance test criterion: we know what level of accuracy represents the model is excellent. After cross-checking, the average network can reach 84% accuracy, and the highest can reach 88%. For more details on the dataset, please visit the UCI Machine Learning website.

Simple Neural Networks

Create a simple neural network and try it out. Import all libraries and functions:

```
import numpy

import pandas

from keras.models import Sequential
```

```
from keras.layers import Dense

from keras.wrappers.scikit_learn import KerasClassifier

from sklearn.cross_validation import cross_val_score

from sklearn.preprocessing import LabelEncoder

from sklearn.cross_validation import StratifiedKFold

from sklearn.preprocessing import StandardScaler

from sklearn.pipeline import Pipeline
```

Initialize the random number seed so that the result is the same every time, helping debug:

```
# fix random seed for reproducibility

seed = 7

numpy.random.seed(seed)
```

Read data with pandas: the first 60 columns are input variables (X), and the last column is output variables (Y). pandas handles data with characters more easily than NumPy.

```
# load dataset

dataframe = pandas.read_csv("sonar.csv", header=None)

dataset = dataframe.values

# split into input (X) and output (Y) variables

X = dataset[:,0:60].astype(float)
```

Y = dataset[:,60]

The output variable is now a string: it needs to be encoded into the numbers 0 and 1. What Scikit-learn LabelEncodercan do is: first fit()import the data by method, then use transform()function coding to add a column:

```
# encode class values as integers

encoder = LabelEncoder()

encoder.fit(Y)

encoded_Y = encoder.transform(Y)
```

It is now possible to create neural network models with Keras. We use Scikit-learn for random K-fold verification and test the model effect. Keras's model KerasClassifiercan be called in Scikit-learn after encapsulation, and the model created by the variables taken; other variables will be passed into the fit()method, such as the number of training times and batch size. We write a function to create this model: there is only one fully connected layer, and the number of neurons is the same as the number of input variables as the most basic model.

The weight of the model is a small Gaussian random number, the activation function is a rectification function, the output layer has only one neuron, and the activation function is an S-type function, which represents the probability of a certain class. The loss function is also a logarithmic loss function (binary cross-entropy), which is suitable for binary classification problems. The optimization algorithm is Adam stochastic gradient descent, and the accuracy of the model is collected every round.

```
# baseline model
```

```python
def create_baseline():

# create model

    model = Sequential()

    model.add(Dense(60, input_dim=60, init='normal',
activation='relu')) model.add(Dense(1, init='normal',
activation='sigmoid'))

# Compile model

        model.compile(loss='binary_crossentropy',
        optimizer='adam', metrics=['accuracy']) return model
```

Test the model with scikit-learn. To KerasClassifierpass training times (default value), close the log:

evaluate model with standardized dataset

```python
    estimator   =   KerasClassifier(build_fn=create_baseline,
    nb_epoch=100, batch_size=5, verbose=0)

    kfold   =   StratifiedKFold(y=encoded_Y,   n_folds=10,
    shuffle=True, random_state=seed)

    results = cross_val_score(estimator, X, encoded_Y, cv=kfold)

    print("Results: %.2f%% (%.2f%%)" % (results.mean()*100,
    results.std()*100))
```

The output is the mean and standard deviation of the test.

    Baseline: 81.68% (5.67%)

It doesn't have to be tired or troublesome, and the effect can be very good.

Preprocessing Data to Increase Performance

It is good practice to pre-process the data. Neural networks like the proportion and distribution of input types to be consistent. To achieve this, regularization can be used. The average value of the data is 0 and the standard deviation is 1. This can preserve the distribution of the data.

scikit-learn StandardScalercan do this. Regularization should not be directly applied to the entire data set: regularization should only be performed when cross-validation on test data, so that regularization becomes a part of cross-validation, so that the model has no prior knowledge of new data and prevents the model from diverging.

scikit-learn Pipelinecan do this directly. Let's define one StandardScalerand then verify:

```
# evaluate baseline model with standardized dataset

numpy.random.seed(seed)

estimators = []

estimators.append(('standardize', StandardScaler()))

estimators.append(('mlp',
KerasClassifier(build_fn=create_baseline, nb_epoch=100,

        batch_size=5, verbose=0)))

pipeline = Pipeline(estimators)
```

```
kfold = StratifiedKFold(y=encoded_Y, n_folds=10,
shuffle=True, random_state=seed)

results = cross_val_score(pipeline, X, encoded_Y, cv=kfold)

print("Standardized: %.2f%% (%.2f%%)" %
(results.mean()*100, results.std()*100))
```

The results are as follows, with a slight improvement in the average effect.

Standardized: 84.07% (6.23%)

Adjusting the Topology and Neurons of the Model

Neural networks have many parameters, such as initialization weights, activation functions, optimization algorithms, and so on. We haven't talked about adjusting the topology of the network: expanding or shrinking the network. Let's experiment:

Shrinking the Network

There may be redundancy in the data: the original data are signals from different angles, and there may be correlations in some of them. Let's reduce the first hidden layer and try to extract features forcibly.

We halved the 60 neurons in the hidden layer of the previous model to 30, so the neural network needs to pick the most important information. The previous regularization works: we also do it together.

```
# smaller model

def create_smaller():

    # create model
```

```python
model = Sequential()

model.add(Dense(30, input_dim=60, init='normal',
activation='relu')) model.add(Dense(1, init='normal',
activation='sigmoid'))

# Compile model

model.compile(loss='binary_crossentropy',
optimizer='adam', metrics=['accuracy']) return model
```

numpy.random.seed(seed)

estimators = []

estimators.append(('standardize', StandardScaler()))

estimators.append(('mlp',
KerasClassifier(build_fn=create_smaller, nb_epoch=100,

batch_size=5, verbose=0)))

pipeline = Pipeline(estimators)

kfold = StratifiedKFold(y=encoded_Y, n_folds=10,
shuffle=True, random_state=seed)

results = cross_val_score(pipeline, X, encoded_Y, cv=kfold)

print("Smaller: %.2f%% (%.2f%%)" % (results.mean()*100,
results.std()*100))

The results are as follows. The average has improved a little, and the variance has been reduced a lot: it really works, because this time it takes only half of the training time!

Smaller: 84.61% (4.65%)

Expanding the Network

After expanding the network, neural networks are more likely to extract key features and combine them in a non-linear manner. Let's simply modify the previous network: add a hidden layer of 30 neurons after the original hidden layer. The current network is:

60 inputs -> [60 -> 30] -> 1 output

We hope that we can model all the variables before reducing the information, similar to the idea of reducing the network. This time we add a layer to help the network select information:

```
# larger model

def create_larger():

    # create model

    model = Sequential()

    model.add(Dense(60, input_dim=60, init='normal',
    activation='relu')) model.add(Dense(30, init='normal',
    activation='relu')) model.add(Dense(1, init='normal',
    activation='sigmoid'))

    # Compile model

    model.compile(loss='binary_crossentropy',
    optimizer='adam', metrics=['accuracy']) return model

numpy.random.seed(seed)

estimators = []

estimators.append(('standardize', StandardScaler()))
```

```
estimators.append(('mlp',
KerasClassifier(build_fn=create_larger, nb_epoch=100,

        batch_size=5, verbose=0)))

pipeline = Pipeline(estimators)

kfold    =    StratifiedKFold(y=encoded_Y,    n_folds=10,
shuffle=True, random_state=seed)

results = cross_val_score(pipeline, X, encoded_Y, cv=kfold)

print("Larger: %.2f%% (%.2f%%)" % (results.mean()*100,
results.std()*100))
```

The results this time were much better and almost reached the best in the industry.

Larger: 86.47% (3.82%)

The results of fine-tuning the network continue to be better. How can you do it?

This project was about developing a binary classification deep learning project using Keras.

- How to import data

- How to create a baseline model

- How to test Keras' model with Scikit-learn through K-fold random cross test

- How to preprocess the data

- How to fine-tune the network

In this section Multi-classification and binary classification are introduced: the next and the final section of this chapter is the regression problem.

Project: Boston Housing Price Returns

This project is about how to solve regression problems with Keras and social networks. This section will illustrate:

- Import CSV data

- Creating a neural network model for regression problems

- Cross-validation of Keras' model using Scikit-learn

- Preprocessing data to increase performance

- Fine-tuning network parameters

let us start.

Boston Housing Price Data

In this chapter, we study the Boston housing price data set, that is, housing information in the Boston area. What we care about is the price of housing, the unit is thousands of dollars: So, this problem is a return issue. The data has 13 input variables, which represent different properties of the house:

1. CRIM: Per capita crime rate

2. ZN: Proportion of civil land above 25,000 square feet

3. INDUS: Proportion of Commercial Land in Urban Non-Retail Industry

4. CHAS: Whether it is adjacent to the Charles River, 1 is adjacent, 0 is not adjacent

5. NOX: Nitric Oxide Concentration (1/10 million)

6. RM: Average number of rooms in a residence

7. AGE: Proportion of Houses Owned and Built Before 1940

8. DIS: Weighted Distance to 5 Boston Career Centers

9. RAD: convenience index to highway

10. TAX: property tax rate per 10,000 dollar

11. PTRATIO: Student-Teacher Ratio in Towns

12. B: 1000 (Bk − 0.63) 2 where Bk is the proportion of blacks in the town

13. LSTAT: Proportion of Low-Income Population

14. MEDV: Median price of self-occupied housing, unit is thousand dollar

This problem has been studied in depth; all data are numbers. The first five rows of the data are:

0.00632 18.00 2.310 0 0.5380 6.5750 65.20 4.0900 1 296.0 15.30 396.90 4.98 24.00

0.02731 0.00 7.070 0 0.4690 6.4210 78.90 4.9671 2 242.0 17.80 396.90 9.14 21.60

0.02729 0.00 7.070 0 0.4690 7.1850 61.10 4.9671 2 242.0 17.80 392.83 4.03 34.70

0.03237 0.00 2.180 0 0.4580 6.9980 45.80 6.0622 3 222.0 18.70 394.63 2.94 33.40

0.06905 0.00 2.180 0 0.4580 7.1470 54.20 6.0622 3 222.0 18.70 396.90 5.33 36.20

The data is in the data directory of this book, or you can download it yourself and rename it housing.csv. The normal model has a mean square error (MSE) of about 20 and a variance (SSE) of $ 4,500. For more details on the dataset, please visit the UCI Machine Learning website.

Simple Neural Network

First, create a simple regression neural network. Import all libraries and functions:

```
import numpy

import pandas

from keras.models import Sequential

from keras.layers import Dense

from keras.wrappers.scikit_learn import KerasRegressor

from sklearn.cross_validation import cross_val_score

from sklearn.cross_validation import KFold

from sklearn.preprocessing import StandardScaler

from sklearn.pipeline import Pipeline
```

The source file is in CSV format, and the separator is a space: it can be imported with pandas and then divided into input (X) and output (Y) variables.

```
# load dataset

dataframe = pandas.read_csv("housing.csv",
delim_whitespace=True, header=None)

dataset = dataframe.values

# split into input (X) and output (Y) variables

X = dataset[:,0:13]

Y = dataset[:,13]
```

Keras can encapsulate the model and give it to Scikit-learn, which is convenient for testing the model. We write a function to create a neural network.

The code is shown below. There is a fully connected layer, the number of neurons is the same as the number of input variables (13), and the activation function is also a rectification function. There is no activation function in the output layer because, in the regression problem, we want to take the result directly.

The optimization function is Adam, and the loss function is MSE, which is consistent with the function we want to optimize: this way you can intuitively understand the prediction of the model, because the MSE power is the error in thousands of dollars.

```
# define base mode

def baseline_model():
```

```
# create model

model = Sequential()

model.add(Dense(13,  input_dim=13,  init='normal',
activation='relu')) model.add(Dense(1, init='normal'))

# Compile model

model.compile(loss='mean_squared_error',
optimizer='adam') return model
```

Using the KerasRegressorencapsulation model, any other variables
will be passed into the fit()function, such as the number of trainings
and batch size. Here we take the default values. Old rules, in order to
reproduce the results, specify the random number seed:

```
# fix random seed for reproducibility

seed = 7

numpy.random.seed(seed)

# evaluate model with standardized dataset

estimator    =    KerasRegressor(build_fn=baseline_model,
nb_epoch=100, batch_size=5, verbose=0)
```

You can test the results of the benchmark model: take a 10-fold cross-
check to see.

```
kfold = KFold(n=len(X), n_folds=10, random_state=seed)

results = cross_val_score(estimator, X, Y, cv=kfold)
```

```
print("Results:  %.2f  (%.2f)  MSE" % (results.mean(),
results.std()))
```

The result is the mean and standard deviation of the 10 tests.

```
Results: 38.04 (28.15) MSE
```

Preprocessing Data to Increase Performance

The characteristic of this data set is that the scales of the variables are inconsistent, so normalization is useful.

scikit-learn Pipelinecan be directly homogenized and cross-checked so that the model does not know the new data in advance. code show as below:

```
# evaluate model with standardized dataset

numpy.random.seed(seed)

estimators = []

estimators.append(('standardize', StandardScaler()))

estimators.append(('mlp',
KerasRegressor(build_fn=baseline_model, nb_epoch=50,

        batch_size=5, verbose=0)))

pipeline = Pipeline(estimators)

kfold = KFold(n=len(X), n_folds=10, random_state=seed)

results = cross_val_score(pipeline, X, Y, cv=kfold)

print("Standardized: %.2f (%.2f) MSE" % (results.mean(),
results.std()))
```

The effect is directly better than 10,000 knives:

Standardized: 28.24 (26.25) MSE

You can also normalize the data and use the S-shaped function as the activation function in the last layer to pull the proportions to the same.

Adjusting the Topology of the Model

Neural networks have many adjustable parameters: the most playable is the structure of the network. This time we try with a deeper and wider model.

Deeper Models

Increasing the number of layers of the neural network can improve the effect, so that the model can extract and combine more features. We try to add a few hidden layers: just a few words. Copy the code from above, add a hidden layer after the first layer, and the number of neurons is half of the upper layer:

```
def larger_model():

    # create model

    model = Sequential()

    model.add(Dense(13,  input_dim=13,  init='normal',
    activation='relu'))  model.add(Dense(6,  init='normal',
    activation='relu')) model.add(Dense(1, init='normal'))

    # Compile model

    model.compile(loss='mean_squared_error',
    optimizer='adam') return model
```

This structure is:

13 inputs -> [13 -> 6] -> 1 output

The test method is the same, and the data is regularized:

```
numpy.random.seed(seed)

estimators = []

estimators.append(('standardize', StandardScaler()))

estimators.append(('mlp',
KerasRegressor(build_fn=larger_model, nb_epoch=50,
batch_size=5,

        verbose=0)))

pipeline = Pipeline(estimators)

kfold = KFold(n=len(X), n_folds=10, random_state=seed)

results = cross_val_score(pipeline, X, Y, cv=kfold)

print("Larger: %.2f (%.2f) MSE" % (results.mean(),
results.std()))
```

The effect is a bit better, MSE changed from 28 to 24:

Larger: 24.60 (25.65) MSE

Wider Model

Widening the model can increase network capacity. We subtract one layer and increase the number of neurons in the hidden layer from 13 to 20:

```python
def wider_model():

    # create model

    model = Sequential()

    model.add(Dense(20, input_dim=13, init='normal',
activation='relu')) model.add(Dense(1, init='normal'))

    # Compile model

    model.compile(loss='mean_squared_error',
    optimizer='adam') return model
```

The structure of the network is:

```
13 inputs -> [20] -> 1 output
```

Run and try:

```python
numpy.random.seed(seed)

estimators = []

estimators.append(('standardize', StandardScaler()))

estimators.append(('mlp',
KerasRegressor(build_fn=wider_model,       nb_epoch=100,
batch_size=5,

        verbose=0)))

pipeline = Pipeline(estimators)

kfold = KFold(n=len(X), n_folds=10, random_state=seed)

results = cross_val_score(pipeline, X, Y, cv=kfold)
```

```
print("Wider:    %.2f   (%.2f)   MSE"   %   (results.mean(),
results.std()))
```

The MSE dropped to 21, and it worked well.

Wider: 21.64 (23.75) MSE

It's hard to think that widening the model is better than deepening it: this is the power of Ou Huang.

This project is about developing regression deep learning projects with Keras.

- How to import data

- How to preprocess data to improve performance

- How to adjust the network structure to improve performance

This project concludes the third chapter of this book: you can deal with general machine learning problems now. In the next chapter, we use some tricks to use some high-level APIs of Keras.

Chapter Five

FIVE: KERAS AND ADVANCED MULTILAYER PERCEPTRON

Saving Models with Serialization

Deep learning models may take several days to train well. If you don't have an SL Dafa, you are finished. This very first section of this chapter is about how to save and load models. This chapter will:

- Save model using HDF5 format

- Save model using JSON format

- Save model using the YAML format

let us start.

In Keras, the structure of the model and the weight data are separate: the file format of the weights is HDF5, which is a very efficient way to save a number matrix. The structure of the model is imported and exported using JSON or YAML.

This chapter includes how to modify the HDF5 file manually. The model used is the Pima diabetes model in Chapter 7.

HDF5 File

Hierarchical data format, version 5 (HDF5), can efficiently save large real number matrices, such as neural network weights. HDF5 package needs to be installed:

> sudo pip install h5py

Using JSON to Save Network Structure

The format of JSON is very simple. Keras can to_json()export the model to JSON format and then model_from_json()load it back.

The model and weights need to be compiled once after loading for Keras to call the backend correctly. The verification method of the model is the same as before:

Export:

```python
# MLP for Pima Indians Dataset serialize to JSON and HDF5

from keras.models import Sequential

from keras.layers import Dense

from keras.models import model_from_json

import numpy

import os

# fix random seed for reproducibility

seed = 7

numpy.random.seed(seed)
```

```python
# load pima indians dataset

dataset = numpy.loadtxt("pima-indians-diabetes.csv",
delimiter=",")

# split into input (X) and output (Y) variables

X = dataset[:,0:8]

Y = dataset[:,8]

# create model

model = Sequential()

model.add(Dense(12, input_dim=8, init='uniform',
activation='relu')) model.add(Dense(8, init='uniform',
activation='relu'))

model.add(Dense(1, init='uniform', activation='sigmoid'))

# Compile model

model.compile(loss='binary_crossentropy', optimizer='adam',
metrics=['accuracy']) # Fit the model

model.fit(X, Y, nb_epoch=150, batch_size=10, verbose=0)

# evaluate the model

scores = model.evaluate(X, Y, verbose=0)

print("%s: %.2f%%" % (model.metrics_names[1],
scores[1]*100))

# serialize model to JSON
```

```python
model_json = model.to_json()

with open("model.json", "w") as json_file:

    json_file.write(model_json)

# serialize weights to HDF5

model.save_weights("model.h5")

print("Saved model to disk"
```

Import:

```python
# later...

# load json and create model

# MLP for Pima Indians Dataset serialize to JSON and HDF5

from keras.models import Sequential

from keras.layers import Dense

from keras.models import model_from_json

import numpy

import os

# fix random seed for reproducibility

seed = 7

numpy.random.seed(seed)

# load pima indians dataset
```

```python
dataset = numpy.loadtxt("pima-indians-diabetes.csv",
delimiter=",")

# split into input (X) and output (Y) variables

X = datasct[:,0:8]

Y = dataset[:,8]

# create model

model = Sequential()

model.add(Dense(12, input_dim=8, init='uniform',
activation-'relu')) model.add(Dense(8, init='uniform',
activation='relu'))

model.add(Dense(1, init='uniform', activation='sigmoid'))

# Compile model

model.compile(loss='binary_crossentropy', optimizer='adam',
metrics=['accuracy']) # Fit the model

model.fit(X, Y, nb_epoch=150, batch_size=10, verbose=0)

# evaluate the model

scores = model.evaluate(X, Y, verbose=0)

print("%s: %.2f%%" % (model.metrics_names[1],
scores[1]*100))

# serialize model to JSON

model_json = model.to_json()
```

```
with open("model.json", "w") as json_file:

json_file.write(model_json)

# serialize weights to HDF5

model.save_weights("model.h5")

print("Saved model to disk")

# later...

# load json and create model
```

The results are as follows. The imported model is the same as the previous export:

acc: 79.56%

Saved model to disk

Loaded model from disk

acc: 79.56%

The JSON file is similar:

```
{

    "class_name": "Sequential",

    "config": [{

    "class_name": "Dense",

    "config": {
```

"W_constraint": null,

"b_constraint": null,

"name": "dense_1",

"output_dim": 12,

"activity_regularizer": null,

"trainable": true,

"init": "uniform",

"input_dtype": "float32",

"input_dim": 8,

"b_regularizer": null,

"W_regularizer": null,

"activation": "relu",

"batch_input_shape": [

        null,

        8

]

}

},

{

"class_name": "Dense",

"config": {

"W_constraint": null,

"b_constraint": null,

"name": "dense_2",

"activity_regularizer": null,

"trainable": true,

"init": "uniform",

"input_dim": null,

"b_regularizer": null,

"W_regularizer": null,

"activation": "relu",

"output_dim": 8

}

},

{

 "class_name": "Dense",

"config": {

"W_constraint": null,

"b_constraint": null,

"name": "dense_3",

"activity_regularizer": null,

"trainable": true,

"init": "uniform",

"input_dim": null,

"b_regularizer": null,

"W_regularizer": null,

 "activation": "sigmoid",

"output_dim": 1

}

}

]

}

Using YAML to Save Network Structure

Similar to the previous JSON, except that the file format becomes YAML, and the functions used become to_yaml() and model_from_yaml():

```
# MLP for Pima Indians Dataset serialize to YAML and
HDF5
```

```python
from keras.models import Sequential

from keras.layers import Dense

from keras.models import model_from_yaml

import numpy

import os

# fix random seed for reproducibility

seed = 7

numpy.random.seed(seed)

# load pima indians dataset

dataset = numpy.loadtxt("pima-indians-diabetes.csv",
delimiter=",")

# split into input (X) and output (Y) variables

X = dataset[:,0:8]

Y = dataset[:,8]

# create model

model = Sequential()

model.add(Dense(12, input_dim=8, init='uniform',
activation='relu')) model.add(Dense(8, init='uniform',
activation='relu'))

model.add(Dense(1, init='uniform', activation='sigmoid'))
```

```python
# Compile model

model.compile(loss='binary_crossentropy', optimizer='adam', metrics=['accuracy']) # Fit the model

model.fit(X, Y, nb_epoch=150, batch_size=10, verbose=0)

# evaluate the model

scores = model.evaluate(X, Y, verbose=0)

print("%s: %.2f%%" % (model.metrics_names[1], scores[1]*100))

# serialize model to YAML

model_yaml = model.to_yaml()

with open("model.yaml", "w") as yaml_file:

        yaml_file.write(model_yaml)

# serialize weights to HDF5

model.save_weights("model.h5")

print("Saved model to disk")

# later...

# load YAML and create model

yaml_file = open('model.yaml', 'r') loaded_model_yaml = yaml_file.read() yaml_file.close()

loaded_model = model_from_yaml(loaded_model_yaml) # load weights into new model
```

```
loaded_model.load_weights("model.h5") print("Loaded
model from disk")

# evaluate loaded model on test data

loaded_model.compile(loss='binary_crossentropy',
optimizer='rmsprop', metrics=['accuracy']) score =
loaded_model.evaluate(X, Y, verbose=0)

print "%s: %.2f%%" % (loaded_model.metrics_names[1],
score[1]*100)
```

The result is the same as before:

acc: 79.56%

Saved model to disk

Loaded model from disk

acc: 79.56%

The YAML file looks like this:

class_name: Sequential

config:

- class_name: Dense

config:

W_constraint: null

W_regularizer: null

activation: relu

activity_regularizer: null

b_constraint: null

b_regularizer: null

batch_input_shape: !!python/tuple [null, 8]

init: uniform

input_dim: 8

input_dtype: float32

name: dense_1

output_dim: 12

trainable: true

- class_name: Dense

config: {W_constraint: null, W_regularizer: null, activation: relu, activity_regularizer:

null,

b_constraint: null, b_regularizer: null, init: uniform, input_dim: null, name: dense_2,

output_dim: 8, trainable: true}

- class_name: Dense

config: {W_constraint: null, W_regularizer: null, activation: sigmoid, activity_regularizer: null,

b_constraint: null, b_regularizer: null, init: uniform,
input_dim: null, name: dense_3,

output_dim: 1, trainable: true}

This section was about importing and exporting Keras models.

- How to save loading weights with HDF5

- How to save and load models with JSON

- How to save and load models with YAML

The model is ready to be saved: the next section is about using savepoints.

Using Save Points to Save the Best Model

Deep learning may take a long time to run, and if it breaks in the middle (especially when running on a bidding instance), it will be personal. This section is about saving models halfway through training. This chapter will:

- Save points are important!

- Save points every round!

- Pick the best model!

Let us start.

Using Savepoints

Long-running programs need to be able to be saved halfway through and be robust. The saved program should continue to run or run directly. The save points of deep learning are used to store the weights of the model: this can continue training or start prediction directly.

Keras has a callback API, which ModelCheckpointcan save network information every round, and can define file locations, file names, and save timings. For example, the loss function or accuracy is saved when it reaches a certain standard, and the format of the file name can include time and accuracy. ModelCheckpointYou needs to pass in the fit()function, and you need to install the h5pylibrary.

Save for Better Results

Good habit: save each round if the effect gets better. Still, use the model from Chapter 7 and test it with 33% of the data.

Verify on the test data set after each round, and save the weights if it performs better than before (monitor = 'val_acc', mode = 'max'). The file name format is weights-improvement-val_acc=.2f.hdf5.

```
# Checkpoint the weights when validation accuracy improves

from keras.models import Sequential

from keras.layers import Dense

from keras.callbacks import ModelCheckpoint

import matplotlib.pyplot as plt

import numpy

# fix random seed for reproducibility
```

```python
seed = 7

numpy.random.seed(seed)

# load pima indians dataset

dataset = numpy.loadtxt("pima-indians-diabetes.csv",
delimiter=",")

# split into input (X) and output (Y) variables

X = dataset[:,0:8]

Y = dataset[:,8]

# create model

model = Sequential()

model.add(Dense(12, input_dim=8, init='uniform',
activation='relu'))

model.add(Dense(8, init='uniform', activation='relu'))

model.add(Dense(1, init='uniform', activation='sigmoid'))

# Compile model

model.compile(loss='binary_crossentropy', optimizer='adam',
metrics=['accuracy'])

# checkpoint

filepath="weights-improvement-{epoch:02d}-
{val_acc:.2f}.hdf5"
```

```
checkpoint = ModelCheckpoint(filepath, monitor='val_acc',
verbose=1, save_best_only=True,

mode='max')

callbacks_list = [checkpoint]

# Fit the model

model.fit(X, Y, validation_split=0.33, nb_epoch=150,
batch_size=10,

callbacks=callbacks_list, verbose=0)
```

The output is as follows: If the effect is better, save it.

```
Epoch 00134: val_acc did not improve

Epoch 00135: val_acc did not improve

Epoch 00136: val_acc did not improve

Epoch 00137: val_acc did not improve

Epoch 00138: val_acc did not improve

Epoch 00139: val_acc did not improve

Epoch 00140: val_acc improved from 0.83465 to 0.83858,
saving the model to

weights-improvement-140-0.84.hdf5

Epoch 00141: val_acc did not improve

Epoch 00142: val_acc did not improve
```

Epoch 00143: val_acc did not improve

Epoch 00144: val_acc did not improve

Epoch 00145: val_acc did not improve

Epoch 00146: val_acc improved from 0.83858 to 0.84252, saving model to

weights-improvement-146-0.84.hdf5

Epoch 00147: val_acc did not improve

Epoch 00148: val_acc improved from 0.84252 to 0.84252, saving model to

weights-improvement-148-0.84.hdf5

Epoch 00149: val_acc did not improve

Each model will be saved in the directory:

weights-improvement-74-0.81.hdf5

weights-improvement-81-0.82.hdf5

weights-improvement-91-0.82.hdf5

weights-improvement-93-0.83.hdf5

This method works, but there are many files. Of course, the best model must have survived.

Saving the Best Model

You can also just save the best model: every time if the effect is better, overwrite the previous weight file, and change the previous file name to a fixed one:

```
# Checkpoint the weights for best model on validation accuracy

from keras.models import Sequential

from keras.layers import Dense

from keras.callbacks import ModelCheckpoint

import matplotlib.pyplot as plt

import numpy

# fix random seed for reproducibility

seed = 7

numpy.random.seed(seed)

# load pima indians dataset

dataset = numpy.loadtxt("pima-indians-diabetes.csv", delimiter=",")

# split into input (X) and output (Y) variables

X - datasct[:,0:8]

Y = dataset[:,8]

# create model
```

```
model = Sequential()

model.add(Dense(12, input_dim=8, init='uniform',
activation='relu')) model.add(Dense(8, init='uniform',
activation='relu')) model.add(Dense(1, init='uniform',
activation='sigmoid'))

# Compile model

model.compile(loss='binary_crossentropy', optimizer='adam',
metrics=['accuracy'])

# checkpoint

filepath="weights.best.hdf5"

checkpoint = ModelCheckpoint(filepath, monitor='val_acc',
verbose=1, save_best_only=True,

mode='max')

callbacks_list = [checkpoint]

# Fit the model

model.fit(X, Y, validation_split=0.33, nb_epoch=150,
batch_size=10,

callbacks=callbacks_list, verbose=0)
```

The results are as follows:

```
Epoch 00136: val_acc did not improve

Epoch 00137: val_acc did not improve
```

Epoch 00138: val_acc did not improve

Epoch 00139: val_acc did not improve

Epoch 00140: val_acc improved from 0.83465 to 0.83858, saving model to weights.best.hdf5

Epoch 00141: val_acc did not improve

Epoch 00142: val_acc did not improve

Epoch 00143: val_acc did not improve

Epoch 00144: val_acc did not improve

Epoch 00145: val_acc did not improve

Epoch 00146: val_acc improved from 0.83858 to 0.84252, saving model to weights.best.hdf5

Epoch 00147: val_acc did not improve

Epoch 00148: val_acc improved from 0.84252 to 0.84252, saving model to weights.best.hdf5

Epoch 00149: val_acc did not improve

The network is stored in:

weights.best.hdf5

Importing a Saved Model

Savepoints only save weights, and the network structure needs to be saved in advance. See Chapter 13, the code is as follows:

How to load and use weights from a checkpoint

```python
from keras.models import Sequential

from keras.layers import Dense

from keras.callbacks import ModelCheckpoint

 import matplotlib.pyplot as plt

import numpy

# fix random seed for reproducibility

seed = 7

numpy.random.seed(seed)

# create model

model = Sequential()

model.add(Dense(12, input_dim=8, init='uniform',
activation='relu')) model.add(Dense(8, init='uniform',
activation='relu'))

model.add(Dense(1, init='uniform', activation='sigmoid'))

# load weights

model.load_weights("weights.best.hdf5")

# Compile model (required to make predictions)
model.compile(loss='binary_crossentropy', optimizer='adam',
metrics=['accuracy']) print("Created model and loaded
weights from file")

# load pima indians dataset
```

```
dataset = numpy.loadtxt("pima-indians-diabetes.csv",
delimiter=",")

# split into input (X) and output (Y) variables

X = dataset[:,0:8]

Y = dataset[:,8]

# estimate accuracy on whole dataset using loaded weights

scores = model.evaluate(X, Y, verbose=0)

print("%s: %.2f%%" % (model.metrics_names[1],
scores[1]*100))
```

The results are as follows:

Created model and loaded weights from file

acc: 77.73%

This section was about saving checkpoints during training.

- How to save the network during optimization

- How to save the best network

- How to import the network

We have learned to create savepoints in this section, and in the next section is about drawing performance charts during training.

Visualization of Model Training Effects

It's helpful to look at historical data on training performance. This section is about visualizing the training effect of the model. This section teaches you:

- How to observe historical training data

- How to draw data accuracy images while training

- How to draw loss images while training

let us start.

Fetching Historical Data

The previous chapter mentioned that Keras supports a callback API, which calls Historyfunctions by default and collects loss and accuracy for each round of training. If there is a test set, it will also collect data from the test set.

Historical data will collect fit()the return value of the function in the history object. Take a look at what data was collected:

```
# list all data in history

print(history.history.keys())
```

If it is the binary classification problem of Chapter 7:

```
['acc', 'loss', 'val_acc', 'val_loss']
```

You can use this data to draw a line chart and visually see:

- Speed of model convergence (slope)

- Whether the model has converged (stability)

- Whether the model is overfitting (validating the data set)

And much more.

Visual Keras Model Training

Collect historical data from Chapter 7 of the Pima diabetes model and plot:

1. Training and validation set accuracy

2. Loss of training and validation set

```
# Visualize training history

from keras.models import Sequential

from keras.layers import Dense

import matplotlib.pyplot as plt

import numpy

# fix random seed for reproducibility

seed = 7

numpy.random.seed(seed)

# load pima indians dataset

dataset = numpy.loadtxt("pima-indians-diabetes.csv",
delimiter=",")

# split into input (X) and output (Y) variables
```

```python
X = dataset[:,0:8]

Y = dataset[:,8]

# create model

model = Sequential()

model.add(Dense(12, input_dim=8, init='uniform',
activation='relu'))

model.add(Dense(8, init='uniform', activation='relu'))

model.add(Dense(1, init='uniform', activation='sigmoid'))

# Compile model

model.compile(loss='binary_crossentropy', optimizer='adam',
metrics=['accuracy'])

# Fit the model

history = model.fit(X, Y, validation_split=0.33, nb_epoch=150,
batch_size=10, verbose=0) # list all data in history

print(history.history.keys())

# summarize history for accuracy

plt.plot(history.history['acc'])

plt.plot(history.history['val_acc'])

plt.title('model accuracy')

plt.ylabel('accuracy')
```

plt.xlabel('epoch')

plt.legend(['train', 'test'], loc='upper left') plt.show()

# summarize history for loss plt.plot(history.history['loss'])
plt.plot(history.history['val_loss']) plt.title('model loss')

plt.ylabel('loss')

plt.xlabel('epoch')

plt.legend(['train', 'test'], loc='upper left') plt.show()

In this section, we have learned drawing images during training.

- How to look at historic objccts

- How to draw historical performance

- How to plot the different performance of two datasets

Dropout can effectively prevent overfitting: the next section is on this technique, how to implement it in Keras, and best practices.

Using Dropout Regularization to Prevent Overfitting

Dropout is simple, but it can effectively prevent overfitting. This section is about how to use Dropout in Keras. This chapter includes:

- The principle of dropout

- Use of dropout

- Using dropout on hidden layers

let us start.

Dropout Regularization

Programmers such as Srivastava and others have proposed Dropout regularization in their 2014 paper, "Dropout: A Simple Way to Prevent Neural Networks from Overfitting." Dropout means: randomly ignore a part of neurons during each training; these neurons are dropped-out. In other words, these neurons' influence on downstream initiation during forwarding propagation is ignored, and weights are not updated during backward propagation.

The so-called "learning" of a neural network refers to the characteristics that make the weight of each neuron meet the needs. Different neurons can be combined to distinguish certain features of the data. The neighbor of each neuron will depend on the characteristics of the neighbor's behavior. If it depends too much, it will cause overfitting. If you randomly remove a part of the neurons each time, the remaining neurons need to supplement the function of the disappearing neurons, and the entire network becomes a collection of many independent networks (different solutions to the same problem).

The effect of Dropout is that the network is less sensitive to changes in the weight of a certain neuron, increasing the generalization ability, and reducing overfitting.

Using Dropout Regularization in Keras

Dropout is to take a part of neurons with probability in each training, and only use it during training. We will explore other usages later.

The following example is a sonar dataset (Chapter 11), using scikit-learn to perform a 10-fold cross-check, so you can see the difference. There are 60 input variables and one output, and the data is regularized. The baseline model has 2 hidden layers, the first with 60 neurons and the second with 30 neurons. The training method is stochastic gradient descent with low learning rate and momentum. Here is the code for the baseline model:

```
import numpy

import pandas

from keras.models import Sequential

from keras.layers import Dense

from keras.layers import Dropout

from keras.wrappers.scikit_learn import KerasClassifier

from keras.constraints import maxnorm

from keras.optimizers import SGD

from sklearn.cross_validation import cross_val_score

from sklearn.preprocessing import LabelEncoder

from sklearn.cross_validation import StratifiedKFold

from sklearn.preprocessing import StandardScaler

from sklearn.grid_search import GridSearchCV

from sklearn.pipeline import Pipeline

# fix random seed for reproducibility

seed = 7

numpy.random.seed(seed)
```

```python
# load dataset
dataframe = pandas.read_csv("sonar.csv", header=None)
dataset = dataframe.values
# split into input (X) and output (Y) variables
X = dataset[:,0:60].astype(float)
Y = dataset[:,60]
# encode class values as integers
encoder = LabelEncoder()
encoder.fit(Y)
encoded_Y = encoder.transform(Y)


# baseline
def create_baseline():
# create model
model = Sequential()
model.add(Dense(60, input_dim=60, init='normal',
activation='relu')) model.add(Dense(30, init='normal',
activation='relu')) model.add(Dense(1, init='normal',
activation='sigmoid'))
# Compile model
```

```python
sgd = SGD(lr=0.01, momentum=0.8, decay=0.0,
nesterov=False)

model.compile(loss='binary_crossentropy', optimizer=sgd,
metrics=['accuracy'])

return model

numpy.random.seed(seed)

estimators = []

estimators.append(('standardize', StandardScaler()))

estimators.append(('mlp',
KerasClassifier(build_fn=create_baseline, nb_epoch=300,

batch_size=16, verbose=0)))

pipeline = Pipeline(estimators)

kfold = StratifiedKFold(y=encoded_Y, n_folds=10,
shuffle=True, random_state=seed)

results = cross_val_score(pipeline, X, encoded_Y, cv=kfold)

print("Accuracy: %.2f%% (%.2f%%)" %
(results.mean()*100, results.std()*100))
```

The accuracy without Dropout is 82%.

Accuracy: 82.68% (3.90%)

Using Dropout Regularization on the Input Layer

You can use Dropout for the surface layer: Here we use Dropout for the input layer (surface layer) and the first hidden layer, the ratio is 20%, which means that every five inputs per round of training remove one variable randomly.

The original paper recommended limiting the weight of each layer to ensure that the modulus does not exceed 3: it W_constraintcan be used when defining a fully connected layer . The learning rate is increased by 10 times, and the momentum is increased to 0.9, which is also recommended in the original paper. Modify the above model:

```
# dropout in the input layer with weight constraint

def create_model1():

# create model

model = Sequential()

model.add(Dropout(0.2, input_shape=(60,)))

model.add(Dense(60, init='normal', activation='relu',
W_constraint=maxnorm(3))) model.add(Dense(30,
init='normal', activation='relu', W_constraint=maxnorm(3)))
model.add(Dense(1, init='normal', activation='sigmoid'))

# Compile model

sgd = SGD(lr=0.1, momentum=0.9, decay=0.0,
nesterov=False)

model.compile(loss='binary_crossentropy', optimizer=sgd,
metrics=['accuracy'])
```

```
return model

numpy.random.seed(seed)

estimators = []

estimators.append(('standardize', StandardScaler()))

estimators.append(('mlp',
KerasClassifier(build_fn=create_model1, nb_epoch=300,

batch_size=16, verbose=0)))

pipeline = Pipeline(estimators)

kfold = StratifiedKFold(y=encoded_Y, n_folds=10,
shuffle=True, random_state=seed)

results = cross_val_score(pipeline, X, encoded_Y, cv=kfold)

print("Accuracy: %.2f%% (%.2f%%)" %
(results.mean()*100, results.std()*100))
```

Accuracy increased to 86%:

Accuracy: 86.04% (6.33%)

Using Dropout Regularization for Hidden Layers

Hidden layers can of course also use Dropout. Same as last time, this time with Dropout on both hidden layers, the probability is still 20%:

```
# dropout in hidden layers with weight constraint

def create_model2():
```

```
# create model

model = Sequential()

model.add(Dense(60, input_dim=60, init='normal',
activation='relu',

W_constraint=maxnorm(3)))

model.add(Dropout(0.2))

model.add(Dense(30, init='normal', activation='relu',
W_constraint=maxnorm(3)))

model.add(Dropout(0.2))

model.add(Dense(1, init='normal', activation='sigmoid'))

# Compile model

sgd = SGD(lr=0.1, momentum=0.9, decay=0.0,
nesterov=False)

model.compile(loss='binary_crossentropy', optimizer=sgd,
metrics=['accuracy'])

return model

numpy.random.seed(seed)

estimators = []

estimators.append(('standardize', StandardScaler()))

estimators.append(('mlp',
KerasClassifier(build_fn=create_model2, nb_epoch=300,
```

```
batch_size=16, verbose=0)))

pipeline = Pipeline(estimators)

kfold = StratifiedKFold(y=encoded_Y, n_folds=10,
shuffle=True, random_state=seed)

results = cross_val_score(pipeline, X, encoded_Y, cv=kfold)

print("Accuracy: %.2f%% (%.2f%%)" %
(results.mean()*100, results.std()*100))
```

However, there are no moons, and the effect is even worse. May need more training.

Accuracy: 82.16% (6.16%)

Tips for Using Dropout Regularization

The original paper compared many standard machine learning problems and made the following recommendations:

1. The dropout probability should not be too high, starting from 20% and trying to 50%. Too low probability does not work well, too high probability may cause underfitting.

2. The network must be big. Larger networks are more likely to learn different methods.

3. Each layer does Dropout, including the input layer. Better result.

4. The learning rate (with attenuation) and momentum are larger. Multiply the learning rate by 10 or 100, and set the momentum to 0.9 or 0.99.

5. Limit the weight of each layer. Increasing the learning rate will increase the weight, and it is better to limit the modulus of each layer to 4 or 5.

This section was about using Dropout regularization to avoid overfitting.

- How does Dropout work

- How to use Dropout

- What are the best practices for Dropout

Adjusting the learning rate during training improves performance. The next section will look at the effects of different learning rates and how to use them in Keras.

Learning Speed Design

Neural network training is a difficult optimization problem. Traditional stochastic gradient descent algorithms sometimes work better with a well-designed learning speed. This section includes:

- Reasons for adjusting learning speed

- How to use learning speed that changes over time

- How to use learning speed that varies by number of training

let us start.

Learning Speed

Stochastic gradient descent algorithm combined with the designed speed, can enhance the effect and reduce the training time: it is also called learning speed annealing or variable learning speed. In fact, it is to slowly adjust the learning speed, while the traditional method does not change the learning speed.

The simplest adjustment method is to decrease the learning speed over time. In the beginning, make large adjustments to speed up training, and then slowly fine-tune the performance later. Two simple methods:

- Slowly decrease according to the number of training rounds

- Down to a certain point

Let's explore each.

Ionospheric Classification Dataset

This chapter uses the ionosphere binary classification dataset to study free electrons in the ionosphere. The classification g (good) means there is a structure in the ionosphere; b (bad) means no, and the signal passed through the ionosphere. The data has 34 attributes and 351 data.

The best model under 10% test can reach 94 ~ 98% accuracy. The data is in the data directory of this book, or you can download it yourself and rename it ionosphere.csv. See the UCI Machine Learning website for details on the dataset.

Time-Based Learning Speed Scheduling

Keras has a built-in time-based learning speed scheduler: Keras' stochastic gradient descent SGDclass has decay parameters, and the speed is adjusted according to the following formula:

LearnRate = LearnRate x (1 / 1 + decay x epoch)

The default value is 0: No effect.

LearningRate = 0.1 * 1/(1 + 0.0 * 1)

LearningRate = 0.1

If the attenuation rate is greater than 1, for example 0.001, the effect is:

Epoch Learning Rate

1 0.1

2 0.0999000999

3 0.0997006985

4 0.09940249103

5 0.09900646517

Image to 100 rounds:

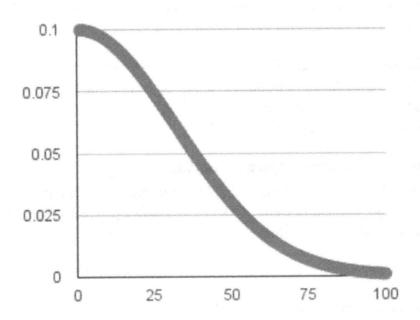

Can be designed like this:

Decay = LearningRate / Epochs

Decay = 0.1 / 100

Decay = 0.001

The following code reduces the learning speed by time. The neural network has 1 hidden layer, 34 neurons, and the activation function is a rectification function. The output layer is a neuron, the activation function is an S-type function, and a probability is output. Set the learning rate to 0.1 and train for 50 rounds. The attenuation rate is 0.002, which is 0.1 / 50. Learning speed adjustment is generally used in conjunction with momentum: momentum is set to 0.8. code show as below:

```
import pandas

import numpy

from keras.models import Sequential

from keras.layers import Dense

from keras.optimizers import SGD

from sklearn.preprocessing import LabelEncoder

# fix random seed for reproducibility

seed = 7

numpy.random.seed(seed)

# load dataset
```

```
dataframe = pandas.read_csv("ionosphere.csv",
header=None)

dataset = dataframe.values

# split into input (X) and output (Y) variables

X = dataset[:,0:34].astype(float)

Y = dataset[:,34]

# encode class values as integers

encoder = LabelEncoder()

encoder.fit(Y)

Y = encoder.transform(Y)

# create model

model = Sequential()

model.add(Dense(34, input_dim=34, init='normal',
activation='relu')) model.add(Dense(1, init='normal',
activation='sigmoid'))

# Compile model

epochs = 50

learning_rate = 0.1

decay_rate = learning_rate / epochs

momentum = 0.8
```

```
sgd = SGD(lr=learning_rate, momentum=momentum,
decay=decay_rate, nesterov=False)
model.compile(loss='binary_crossentropy', optimizer=sgd,
metrics=['accuracy'])

# Fit the model

model.fit(X, Y, validation_split=0.33, nb_epoch=epochs,
batch_size=28)
```

Training 67% and testing 33% of the data, the accuracy reached 99.14%, which is higher than 95.69% without any optimization:

```
235/235 [==============================] - 0s -
loss: 0.0607 - acc: 0.9830 - val_loss:

    0.0732 - val_acc: 0.9914

Epoch 46/50

235/235 [==============================] - 0s -
loss: 0.0570 - acc: 0.9830 - val_loss:

    0.0867 - val_acc: 0.9914

Epoch 47/50

235/235 [==============================] - 0s -
loss: 0.0584 - acc: 0.9830 - val_loss:

    0.0808 - val_acc: 0.9914

Epoch 48/50

235/235 [==============================] - 0s -
loss: 0.0610 - acc: 0.9872 - val_loss:
```

0.0653 - val_acc: 0.9828

Epoch 49/50

235/235 [==============================] - 0s -
loss: 0.0591 - acc: 0.9830 - val_loss:

0.0821 - val_acc: 0.9914

Epoch 50/50

235/235 [==============================] - 0s -
loss: 0.0598 - acc: 0.9872 - val_loss:

0.0739 - val_acc: 0.9914

Learning Speed Scheduling Based on Rounds

You can also fix the schedule: use a certain speed to a certain number of rounds, each time the speed is half of the last time. For example, an initial speed of 0.1 is reduced by half every ten rounds. The drawing is:

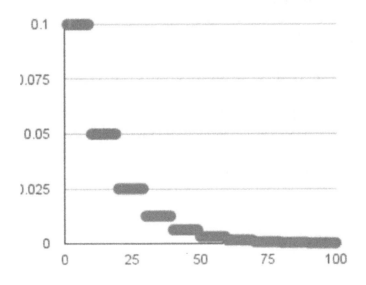

Keras's LearningRateSchedulercallback parameter can control the learning speed, take the current number of rounds, and return to the expected speed. Still the network just now, add a step_decayfunction to generate the following learning rate:

LearnRate = InitialLearningRate x Droprate ^ floor((1+Epoch)/EpochDrop)

InitialLearningRate is the initial speed, DropRate is the deceleration frequency, and how much is reduced by EpochDrop:

import pandas

import pandas

import numpy

import math

from keras.models import Sequential

from keras.layers import Dense

from keras.optimizers import SGD

from sklearn.preprocessing import LabelEncoder

from keras.callbacks import LearningRateScheduler

learning rate schedule

def step_decay(epoch):

  initial_lrate = 0.1

  drop = 0.5

```
    epochs_drop = 10.0

    lrate = initial_lrate * math.pow(drop,
math.floor((1+epoch)/epochs_drop))

    return lrate
```

fix random seed for reproducibility

```
seed = 7

numpy.random.seed(seed)
```

load dataset

```
dataframe = pandas.read_csv("../data/ionosphere.csv",
header=None)

dataset = dataframe.values
```

split into input (X) and output (Y) variables

```
X = dataset[:,0:34].astype(float)

Y = dataset[:,34]
```

encode class values as integers

```
encoder = LabelEncoder()

encoder.fit(Y)

Y = encoder.transform(Y)
```

create model

```
model = Sequential()
```

```
model.add(Dense(34, input_dim=34, init='normal',
activation='relu'))

model.add(Dense(1, init='normal', activation='sigmoid'))

# Compile model

sgd = SGD(lr=0.0, momentum=0.9, decay=0.0,
nesterov=False) model.compile(loss='binary_crossentropy',
optimizer=sgd, metrics=['accuracy'])

# learning schedule callback

lrate = LearningRateScheduler(step_decay)

callbacks_list = [lrate]

# Fit the model

model.fit(X, Y, validation_split=0.33, nb_epoch=50,
batch_size=28, callbacks=callbacks_list)
```

The effect is also 99.14%, which is better than nothing:

```
Epoch 45/50

235/235 [==============================] - 0s -
loss: 0.0546 - acc: 0.9830 - val_loss:

0.0705 - val_acc: 0.9914

Epoch 46/50

235/235 [==============================] - 0s -
loss: 0.0542 - acc: 0.9830 - val_loss:
```

0.0676 - val_acc: 0.9914

Epoch 47/50

235/235 [==============================] - 0s - loss: 0.0538 - acc: 0.9830 - val_loss:

0.0668 - val_acc: 0.9914

Epoch 48/50

235/235 [==============================] - 0s - loss: 0.0539 - acc: 0.9830 - val_loss:

0.0708 - val_acc: 0.9914

Epoch 49/50

235/235 [==============================] - 0s - loss: 0.0539 - acc: 0.9830 - val_loss:

0.0674 - val_acc: 0.9914

Epoch 50/50

235/235 [==============================] - 0s - loss: 0.0531 - acc: 0.9830 - val_loss:

0.0694 - val_acc: 0.9914

Tips for Adjusting Learning Speed

These tips can help tune parameters:

1. Increase initial learning speed. Because the speed will decrease later, the faster the speed, the faster the convergence.

2. Be strong. In this way, if the learning speed decreases in the later period, if the direction is the same, it can continue to converge.

3. Test more. This question is inconclusive and requires more attempts. Also, try exponential drops and do nothing.

This section is about adjusting learning speed.

*   Why adjusting learning speed works

*   How to use time-based learning speed drops in Keras

*   How to write a falling speed function yourself

Chapter 5 ends here, including some advanced functions of Keras and advanced methods of tuning parameters. The next two chapters study Python and Keras Multilayer Neural Networks and Convolutional Neural Networks (CNNs), which are particularly effective in the image and natural language processing.

Chapter Six

PYTHON AND KERAS MULTILAYER NEURAL NETWORKS

In this chapter, you will learn how to implement Multilayer Neural Networks using Python and the Deep Learning Keras library, one of the most popular today.

Keras is a library of Neural Networks, capable of running TensorFlow (not just), and was developed to make prototyping easy and fast.

Multilayered Neural Networks are those in which neurons are structured in two or more layers (layer) processing (as there are at least one layer input and one layer output).

Implementing a complete Neural Networks architecture from scratch is a Herculean task that requires a more solid understanding of Programming, Linear Algebra, and Statistics - not to mention that the computational performance of your implementation will hardly beat the performance of well-known libraries in the community.

To show that with a few lines of code, it is possible to implement a simple network; let's take the well-known MNIST classification problem and see how our algorithm performs when submitted to this 70,000 image dataset!

Neural Network Architecture

Neural Networks are modeled as a set of neurons connected as an acyclic graph. What does this mean in practice? This means that the outputs (outputs) of some neurons are the inputs (inputs) from other neurons.

The most commonly encountered Neural Networks, there are those arranged in layers (layers) different, and each layer containing a set of neurons. The most commonly encountered layer type is that of the fully-connected layer type. In this, neurons between two adjacent layers connect two by two.

This type of architecture is also known as Neural Network Feedforward; it is only allowed to a neuron layer l i connect to a neuron of the layer L i + 1

What is MNIST?

MNIST is a data set that contains thousands of handwritten images from digits 0-9. The challenge with this dataset is, given any image, to apply the corresponding label (correctly classify the image). MNIST is so widely studied and used by the community that it acts as a benchmark for comparing different image recognition algorithms.

The complete dataset consists of 70,000 images, each of 28 X 28 pixels in size. The figure above shows some random copies of the dataset for each of the possible digits. It is noteworthy that the images are already normalized and centralized.

Since images are grayscale, i.e., have only one channel, the value for each pixel in the images should vary within the range [0, 255].

"Multilayer Neural Networks are those in which neurons are structured into two or more processing layers." - IAN GOODFELLOW.

MNIST in Python

Often used, the MNIST dataset is already available inside the library Scikit-learn and can be imported directly by Python com fetch_mldata("MNIST Original").

To illustrate how to import full MNIST and extract some basic information, let's run the code below:

```python
#import the required libraries

from sklearn.datasets import fetch_mldata

import matplotlib.pyplot as plt

import numpy as np


#import the MNIST dataset

dataset = fetch_mldata ("Original MNIST")

(data, labels) = (dataset.data, dataset.target)


# Display some MNIST dataset information

print ("[INFO] Number of images: {}". format (data.shape
[0]))

print ("[INFO] Pixels per image: {}". format (data.shape [1]))


# choose a random dataset index and display

# the corresponding image and label

np.random.seed (17)

randomIndex = np.random.randint (0, data.shape [0])

print ("[INFO] Random MNIST image with label '{: .0f}':".
format (labels [randomIndex]))
```

```
plt.imshow (data [randomIndex] .reshape ((28,28)), cmap =
"Grays")

plt.show ()
```

We will see that the array containing the images has 70,000 rows (one row for each image) and 784 columns (all pixels of the 28 x 28 image). We can also see one of the randomly chosen images. In the case of this digit, our algorithm would have been successful if it could correctly classify the digit as '4'.

Implementing our Neural Network with Python + Keras

Having made a brief introduction about Neural Networks, we will implement a Feedforward Neural Network for the MNIST classification problem.

Create a new file in your favorite IDE, named it rede_neural_keras.py, and follow the code steps below.

```
#import the required packages

from sklearn.datasets import fetch_mldata

from sklearn.model_selection import train_test_split

from sklearn.metrics import classification_report

from sklearn.preprocessing import LabelBinarizer

from keras.models import Sequential

from keras.layers.core import Dense

from keras.optimizers import SGD
```

```
import numpy as np

import matplotlib.pyplot as plt
```

Above, we import all packages needed to create a simple Neural Network with the Keras library. If you have had an error trying to import packages, or do not have a dedicated Python virtual environment for working with Deep Learning / Computer Vision, I recommend looking for a tutorial based on your Operating System.

```
#import MNIST

print ("[INFO] importing MNIST ...")

dataset = fetch_mldata ("Original MNIST")


# normalize all pixels so that the values are

# at intervalor [0, 1.0]

data = dataset.data.astype ("float") / 255.0

labels = dataset.target
```

After importing the image set, I will split it between training set (75%) and test set (25%), a practice well known in the Data Science universe. But beware! The training and testing set MUST be INDEPENDENT, to avoid various problems, including overfitting.

Although it sounds complicated, it can be done with just one line of code, because thanks to the Scikit-learn library, it can be easily done with the method train_test_split.

In this step of preparing our data, we will also need to convert the labels - which are represented by integers - to the binary vector format. To exemplify what a binary vector is, see the example below, which indicates the label '4'.

$$4 = [0.0,0,0,1,0,0,0,0,0]$$

In this vector, the value 1 is assigned to the index corresponding to the label and the value 0 to the others. This operation, known as one-hot encoding, can also be easily done with the class LabelBinarizer.

split dataset between train (75%) and test (25%)

(trainX, testX, trainY, testY) = train_test_split (date, dataset.target)

convert integer labels to vectors

lb = LabelBinarizer ()

trainY = lb.fit_transform (trainY)

testY = lb.transform (testY)

Ready! With the dataset imported and processed correctly, we can finally define the architecture of our Neural Network with Keras.

Arbitrarily, I defined that the Neural Network will have four layers:

Our first layer (l_0) receive as input values for each pixel of the images. That is, as each image has a length of 28 x 28 pixels, l_0 will have 784 neurons.

The hidden layers l_1 and l_2 will have arbitrarily 128 and 64 neurons.

Finally, the last layer L $_3$, have the amount corresponding to the amount neurons classes that our own classification problem: 10 (reminiscent, 10 digits are possible).

```
# define Neural Network architecture using Keras

# 784 (input) = & gt; 128 (hidden) = & gt; 64 (hidden) = & gt; 10 (output)

model = Sequential ()

model.add (Dense (128, input_shape = (784,), activation = "sigmoid"))

model.add (Dense (64, activation = "sigmoid"))

model.add (Dense (10, activation = "softmax"))
```

Within the concept of feedforward architecture, our Neural Network is instantiated by the class Sequential, meaning that each layer will be "stacked" on top of another, with the output of one being the input of the next. In our example, all layers are a fully-connected layer.

The hidden layers will be activated by the function sigmoid, which takes the actual values of the neurons as input and throws them within the range [0, 1]. For the last layer, as this has to reflect the probabilities for each of the possible classes, the function will be used softmax.

To train our model, I will use the most important algorithm for Neural Networks: Stochastic Gradient Descent (SGD). I want to make a dedicated post about SGD in the future (math + code), so important! But for now, let's use the ready algorithm from our libraries.

The SGD learning rate will be 0.01, and the loss function will be a categorical_crossentropy, since the number of output classes is greater than two.

```
# train the model using Stochastic Gradient Descent (SGD)

print ("[INFO] training the neural network ...")

model.compile (optimizer = SGD (0.01), loss =
"categorical_crossentropy",

        metrics = ["accuracy"])

H = model.fit (trainX, trainY, batch_size = 128, epochs = 10,
verbose = 2,

        validation_data = (testX, testY))
```

Deep Learning's strength comes primarily from one very important algorithm: Stochastic Gradient Descent (SGD).

Call the model.fit, then begin the training of the neural network. After a time-varying according to your machine, the weights of each node are optimized, and the network can be considered as trained.

To evaluate the performance of the algorithm, we call the method model.predict to generate predictions on top of the test dataset. The challenge of the model is to forecast the 17,500 images that make up the test suite by assigning a label of 0-9 to each:

```
# evaluate the Neural Network

print ("[INFO] evaluating the neural network ...")

predictions = model.predict (testX, batch_size = 128)
```

```
print (classification_report (testY.argmax (axis = 1),
predictions.argmax (axis = 1)))
```

Finally, after the performance report obtained, we will want to plot accuracy and loss over the iterations. Visually analyzing allows us to easily identify overfitting situations, for example:

```
# plot loss and accuracy for 'train' and 'test' datasets

plt.style.use ("ggplot")

plt.figure ()

plt.plot (np.arange (0.100), H.history ["loss"], label =
"train_loss")

plt.plot (np.arange (0.100), H.history ["val_loss"], label =
"val_loss")

plt.plot (np.arange (0.100), H.history ["acc"], label =
"train_acc")

plt.plot (np.arange (0.100), H.history ["val_acc"], label =
"val_acc")

plt.title ("Training Loss and Accuracy")

plt.xlabel ("Epoch #")

plt.ylabel ("Loss / Accuracy")

plt.legend ()

plt.show ()
```

Running the Neural Network

With the code ready, just run the command below to see our Neural Network built on top of the fully-functioning Keras library:

```
carlos$ python neural_network_keras.py

carlos$ python neural_network_keras.py
```

As a result, its classification_report shows that by the end of the 100 epochs, the network was able to achieve 92% accuracy, which is a good result for this type of architecture. Just as a curiosity, Convolutional Neural Networks have the potential to achieve up to 99% accuracy (!):

Obviously, there are many improvements that can be made to improve the performance of our network, but you can see that even a simple architecture performs very well.

```
                                            2. python3.6
Epoch 94/100
 - 1s - loss: 0.2806 - acc: 0.9196 - val_loss: 0.2853 - val_acc: 0.9158
Epoch 95/100
 - 1s - loss: 0.2795 - acc: 0.9200 - val_loss: 0.2840 - val_acc: 0.9157
Epoch 96/100
 - 1s - loss: 0.2784 - acc: 0.9207 - val_loss: 0.2831 - val_acc: 0.9160
Epoch 97/100
 - 1s - loss: 0.2773 - acc: 0.9206 - val_loss: 0.2821 - val_acc: 0.9163
Epoch 98/100
 - 1s - loss: 0.2762 - acc: 0.9210 - val_loss: 0.2810 - val_acc: 0.9171
Epoch 99/100
 - 1s - loss: 0.2752 - acc: 0.9211 - val_loss: 0.2801 - val_acc: 0.9169
Epoch 100/100
 - 1s - loss: 0.2742 - acc: 0.9210 - val_loss: 0.2790 - val_acc: 0.9177
[INFO] avaliando a rede neural...
             precision    recall  f1-score   support

          0       0.96      0.97      0.96      1815
          1       0.95      0.96      0.96      1927
          2       0.91      0.90      0.91      1787
          3       0.90      0.90      0.90      1754
          4       0.91      0.92      0.92      1684
          5       0.89      0.86      0.88      1624
          6       0.92      0.95      0.94      1737
          7       0.93      0.94      0.93      1781
          8       0.89      0.87      0.88      1674
          9       0.90      0.89      0.90      1717

avg / total       0.92      0.92      0.92     17500
```

We have presented the basic concepts about Neural Networks, as well as the MNIST dataset used to benchmark algorithms.

By testing the performance of a 4-layer neural network (input +2 hidden layers + output), we achieved 92% accuracy in the predictions made.

The implementation was done on top of Keras, to show that with a few lines of code, it is possible to build great classification models.

Chapter Seven

CONVENTIONAL NEURAL NETWORKS WITH PYTHON

In this chapter, I'll show how to implement your first Network Neural Convolutional (Convolutional Neural Network - CNN), inspired by the known neural architecture LeNet-5, and apply it to the dataset ISMN T.

This is a tutorial focused on implementing CNN - that is, I'm assuming you are familiar with the area. For this reason, I will not go into theoretical detail and concepts such as activation functions, Fully-Connected Layer, Pooling Layer, and so on.

MNIST Dataset

In the last chapter, we used the well-known MNIST dataset, which contains thousands of handwritten images from digits 0-9, and created a neural network to classify them.

Briefly, each dataset image is 28 X 28 pixels with grayscale pixel values. As a big advantage, the digits are already normalized (size) and centered.

Sample MNIST dataset.

Since in a grayscale image, the value of each pixel is the only sample of the color space, this value will vary in the range [0, 255], indicating the intensity of that pixel.

Convolutional Neural Networks

Convolutional Neural Networks are a type of neural network that has been successfully applied to Computer Vision problems.

As I said in the introduction, our first CNN implementation will be based on the architecture of LeNet-5, the first CNN implemented and successfully tested!

The choice of this architecture (despite its age) is why this CNN is so didactic! Small and easy to understand, it still gets great results on issues like MNIST. Implementing LeNet-5 is like Hello, World! CNN

189

LeNet-5 Architecture

Proposed by LeCun (1998) in his paper Gradient-Based Learning Applied to Document. Recognition, LeNet-5 focuses on digit recognition and is designed to recognize zip code numbers in matches.

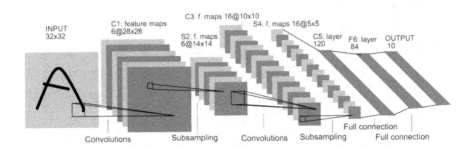

The architecture of LeNet-5, a Convolutional Neural Network (CNN) for digit recognition.

The above figure is the original image of LeCun's paper. In a quick analysis, we see that the past image as input is not flattened (flatten), but is passed preserving its dimensions. This is mandatory to maintain the spatial relationship between its pixels   - a flat image would lose this important information.

You can also see that there are three types of layers:

- Convolutional Layers (CONV);

- Pooling Layers (POOL);

- Fully-Connected Layers (FC).

LeNet - 5

Detailed LeNet-5 architecture.

Briefly, the architecture of LeNet-5 consists of a sequence with the following layers:

- CNN is composed of a set of 6 filters (5×5), stride = 1.

- POOL (2×2), stride = 2, to reduce the spatial size of the resulting matrices.

- CNN (5×5) with 16 filters and stride = 1.

- POOL (2×2) , stride = 2 .

  - The feature maps are flat (flatten), forming 400 knots (5x5x16) for the next command FC.

- FC with 120 knots.

- FC with 84 knots.

If you take a look at the article, you will notice that the activation functions referenced were SIGMOID and TANHin the meantime. I will use activation RELU, which gives us much better accuracy! Another observation at the time the paper was written was that average pooling was used much more than max pooling. In the model that we will implement, I will use max pooling.

Implementing a CNN with Python + Keras

Before entering the code itself, see how the project was split. To keep code organized - after all, there's nothing worse than writing everything in one file! - I created a module cnn containing the LeNet-5 class. CNN's application to the MNIST dataset is in a separate file lenet5_mnist.py. Following is the project structure:

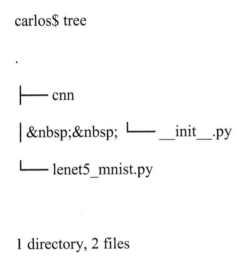

carlos$ tree

.

├── cnn

| └── __init__.py

└── lenet5_mnist.py

1 directory, 2 files

By structuring a project into modules and submodules, you make them easier to scale, and adopt good programming practice and make everything more readable for others.

Writing the LeNet5 Class

Within the module cnn, create a file __init__.py to implement the LeNet5 class. Import the required packages and declare the class:

```
"""
```

It contains CNN architecture implementations.

LeNet5] - CNN inspired by LeCun [1] architecture, with some

changes in the activation, padding, and pooling functions.

1] http://yann.lecun.com/exdb/publis/pdf/lecun-01a.pdf

```
"""
```

```python
# import the necessary packages
from keras.models import Sequential
from keras.layers.core import Flatten
from keras.layers.core import Dense
from keras.layers.convolutional import Conv2D
from keras.layers.convolutional import MaxPooling2D
from keras.layers.core import Activation


class LeNet5(object):
```

"""

LeNet5 architecture with minor changes.

Focusing on digit recognition, this CNN is composed of

by a sequence containing the following layers:

INPUT => CONV => POOL => CONV =>
POOL => FC => FC => OUTPUT

"""

I will define the static method build (using the @staticmethod decorator) within the class LeNet5, so it will not be necessary to instantiate the method. The method is provided with arguments regarding image size, number of channels, and classes, and this will stack the CNN layers, returning the model.

@staticmethod

def build(width, height, channels, classes):

"""

Build a CNN with LeNet5 architecture.

param width: Pixel width of the image.

:param height: Height in pixel of the image.

param channels: Number of image channels.

param classes: Number of classes for the output.

return: Cnn of type LeNet5.

"""

inputShape = (height, width, channels)


```python
model = Sequential()
model.add(Conv2D(6, (5, 5), padding="same",
        input_shape=inputShape))
model.add(Activation("relu"))
model.add(MaxPooling2D((2,2)))
model.add(Conv2D(16, (5, 5))))
model.add(Activation("relu"))
model.add(MaxPooling2D((2,2)))
model.add(Flatten())
model.add(Dense(120))
model.add(Activation("relu"))
model.add(Dense(84))
model.add(Activation("relu"))
```

```python
model.add(Dense(classes))

model.add(Activation("softmax"))


return model
```

The CNN is instantiated by the class Sequential, and each layer is added following the other, following the architecture already detailed above.

Remember that to run Line 48, you must first turn the feature map into a vector with 400 neurons by running Flatten (). On-Line 49, the 84-knot FC will connect to each of the 400 "flattened" nodes.

In the last layer, a size 10 FC type layer is added, which is exactly the number of problem classes. We use the activation function softmax because we want to output the probability associated with each class.

In a nutshell, CNN's architecture looked like this:

INPUT => CONV => POOL => CONV => POOL =>FC => FC => OUTPUT

Only that! The LeNet5 class is 100% implemented, ready to be used not only in MNIST, but any other image classification issue.

Applying CNN to MNIST

In the root directory of your project, create a file lenet5_mnist.py, import the libraries that will be used, and don't forget the newly created class LeNet5. Just as we did in the previous chapter, import and normalize the MNIST dataset:

```
"""
```

Train a CNN with the MNIST dataset.

CNN is inspired by the LeNet-5 architecture, with some changes in the activation, padding, and pooling functions.

"""

```python
# import necessary packages

from keras.utils import to_categorical

from keras.optimizers import SGD

from keras import backend

from sklearn.datasets import fetch_mldata

from sklearn.model_selection import train_test_split

from sklearn.metrics import classification_report

import matplotlib.pyplot as plt

from cnn import LeNet5 # THIS IS THE CLASS CREATED
BY US


# Import and normalize the MNIST dataset

dataset = fetch_mldata("MNIST Original")
```

```python
labels = dataset.target

data = dataset.data.astype("float32") / 255.0
```

Remember the second Figure of this chapter, which shows that the CNN input must be an image with width and height? So when we imported the dataset directly through sklearn, it automatically reduced the dimensions of the images, turning them into a vector with 784 values.

For CNN to work properly, we have to convert this vector to an array of type (28x28x1). This can be easily done by the method reshape:

```python
# converter as imagens de 1D para o formato (28x28x1)

if backend.image_data_format() == "channels_last":

data = data.reshape((data.shape[0], 28, 28, 28, 1)))

senão..:

data = data.reshape((data.shape[0], 1, 28, 28)))
```

An attentive reader will realize that I have two possible situations; my picture can be resized to the shape (28x28x1) or to (1x28x28). This is why Keras for using both Theano and Tensorflow in the backend. As the Theano community uses the channels first ordering and the Tensorflow community is adopted channels last, it is very important to check this to ensure application compatibility.

To find out what you are using on the backend, just take a look at the configuration file ~/.keras/keras.json:

```
carlos$ cat ~/.keras/keras.json

{
```

"epsilon: 1e-07,

"floatx": "float32",

"image_data_format": "channels_last",

"backend": "tensorflow"

The next step is to divide the data set between training (75%) and test (25%) using the method train_test_splitand transform the inner label numbers to train Y and test Y from binary vector format with the aid of the method to_categorical:

Divide the dataset between train (75%) and test (25%)

(trainX, testX, trainY, testY) – train_test_split(data, labels)

Turn labels into binary vectors

trainY = to_categorical(trainY, 10)

testY = to_categorical(testY, 10)

CNN Training

LeNet5 class implemented, input data handled correctly, and now it's time to compile CNN and train it with MNIST digits:

Initialize and optimize model

print("[INFO] initializing and optimizing CNN...")

model = LeNet5.build(28, 28, 1, 10)

```
model.compile(optimizer=SGD(0.01),
loss="categorical_crossentropy",

    metrics=["accuracy"])


# Train CNN

print("[INFO] training CNN...")

H = model.fit(trainX, trainY, batch_size=128, epochs=20,
verbose=2,

    validation_data=(testX, testY))
```

In Line 39, when passing the arguments to the static method LeNet5.build, the LeNet-5 Convolutional Network is assigned to the variable model. I compile the model on Line 40 using the Stochastic Gradient Descent (SGD) algorithm for optimization and loss function equal to categorical_crossentropy, since there are multiple classes in the output.

In Line 45 starts the training of the Neural Convolutional Network, a process that may take a little longer if you are not using any GPU.

Evaluating CNN

To evaluate the performance of our CNN, we call the method model.predict to generate forecasts on top of the test dataset. The challenge of the model is to forecast the 17,500 images that make up the test suite by assigning a label of 0-9 to each:

```
# evaluate CNN

print ("[INFO] evaluating CNN ...")
```

```
predictions = model.predict (testX, batch_size = 64)

print (classification_report (testY.argmax (axis = 1),
predictions.argmax (axis = 1),

            target_names = [str (label) for label in range
(10)]))
```

Finally, after the performance report obtained, we want to plot accuracy and loss over the iterations:

```
# plot loss and accuracy for 'train' and 'test' datasets

plt.style.use ("ggplot")

plt.figure ()

plt.plot (np.arange (0.20), H.history ["loss"], label = "train_loss")

plt.plot (np.arange (0.20), H.history ["val_loss"], label = "val_loss")

plt.plot (np.arange (0.20), H.history ["acc"], label = "train_acc")

plt.plot (np.arange (0.20), H.history ["val_acc"], label = "val_acc")

plt.title ("Training Loss and Accuracy")

plt.xlabel ("Epoch #")

plt.ylabel ("Loss / Accuracy")
```

plt.legend ()

plt.savefig ('cnn.png', bbox_inches = 'tight')

Running CNN LeNet5 MNIST

I ran the script on a p2.xlarge instance of AWS, and it took about one minute for CNN to be trained. This P2 instance uses one NVIDIA K80 GPU and four v CPUs at the cost of $ 0.90 / hour. However, our code runs typically on a non-GPU machine, as it is a small network processing a small dataset.

For comparison, with AWS GPU, it epochs=20took about 60 seconds to train the LeNet-5. My non-GPU machine (CPU only) took 360 seconds.

Go ahead and run lenet5_mnist.py python:

(deeplearning) ubuntu @ ip-xxx-xx-xx-xxx: ~ / sigmoidal / cnn_lenet5 $ python lenet5_mnist.py

Using TensorFlow backend.

[INFO] initializing and optimizing CNN ...

[INFO] training CNN ...

Train on 52500 samples, validate on 17500 samples

Epoch 1/20

9s - loss: 1.3031 - acc: 0.5689 - val_loss: 0.8836 - val_acc: 0.7410

Epoch 2/20

3s - loss: 0.3267 - acc: 0.8990 - val_loss: 0.2708 - val_acc: 0.9147

...

3s - loss: 0.0499 - acc: 0.9846 - val_loss: 0.0584 - val_acc: 0.9814

[INFO] evaluating CNN ...

	precision	recall	f1-score	support
0	0.99	0.99	0.99	1714
1	0.99	0.99	0.99	1958
2	0.98	0.98	0.98	1724
3	0.98	0.98	0.98	1801
4	0.98	0.98	0.98	1703
5	0.99	0.97	0.98	1564
6	0.99	0.99	0.99	1732
7	0.99	0.97	0.98	1794
8	0.97	0.98	0.97	1724
9	0.96	0.98	0.97	1786
avg / total	0.98	0.98	0.98	17500

After all this work, let's take a look at the performance of our first CNN and compare it to the simple neural network we implemented in the previous chapter.

We achieved 98% accuracy in predictions made with trained LeNet-5. Even though it was an old architecture (the first CNN successfully implemented) and without making major changes, it easily beat the performance of the other simple neural network - which had achieved 92% accuracy.

Finally, the script provided the plot of accuracy and loss as a function of the epoch. When we train a Deep Learning model, the graph we expect is that type, training, and validation loss with very similar curves, as well as both accuracy with similar behavior - a pattern that indicates no overfitting.

However, this type of chart is quite difficult to achieve in more complex problems. The MNIST dataset has been largely preprocessed and standardized - and we know that's not what awaits us in the real world - so it makes such a beautiful chart. That is, the preprocessing of your data set is extremely important for algorithm performance.

The LeNet-5 is taken as a network shallow (shallow) as compared to architectures deep (deep) modern. As we have seen, it has only four layers (two CONV and two POOL), little by today's standards. Today, a state-of-the-art architecture can easily exceed 100 layers (like ResNet).

However, we saw that even this simple CNN structure was able to achieve 98% accuracy in the MNIST dataset, making it a great initial example for implementation.

Conclusion

The great advances in the field of Artificial Intelligence in the last two decades are proving essential for the advancement of technology. Mechanisms such as Big Data, Cloud Computing, and the Internet of Things or Machine Learning itself are more than present today for the benefit of anyone and represent the great future of this field for years to come.

The big technology companies have echoed this, and when it comes to Machine Learning and Deep Learning have not been long in coming. Google, Apple, IBM, or Facebook have spent millions of dollars in these years on buying startups and hiring 'gurus' from this field for their investigations.

One of the great advantages of Deep Learning is that it can be applied to functions that have until recently been considered very specific to humans, such as vision or natural language processing. For consumers, this translates into better software, able to sort photos, understand spoken commands, translate text written in other languages, or have our mobile recognize our face.

To conclude this book, I will discuss why you should learn Python and an interesting application of Deep Learning and Python in Space.

Why Should you Start Learning Python Today?

Programming languages have been around for a long time to meet a variety of demands, areas, or to solve specific problems. If you follow this universe, you know that every year, new "trendy" languages emerge, snatching up a lot of developers who want to keep up with the hype.

The number of new languages has brought about a "programming modality," which is actually a joke: Hype Driven Development.

Who is a more experienced programmer can follow, but this amount of languages (C, C ++, Java, JavaScript, Python, Ruby, Matlab, R, among many others) leaves a beginner confused.

After all, like so many options, which one to learn?

There is no better or worse language; all have their applications and strengths/weaknesses. However, to start your career as a data scientist, I recommend you learn Python.

Created in the 1990s by Guido van Rossum, Python is already dominating the world scene. Read in this article its main advantages of this programming language, as well as the course tips that I have separated for you.

Python for Data Science

Python is already the most used language in Data Science; that's a fact. The stakes are to remain in the lead for a long time yet.

There are several reasons why I recommend Python, or you already know several of them. But I want to list here some of the main ones:

- Learning Curve - Python is one of the most accessible, simple, and fast to learn languages - with a few command lines, you can write your scripts.

- Market Demand - A Stack Overflow Survey showed that Python was the fastest growing language in recent years. A projection shows that this trend is expected to intensify in the coming years.

- Growing Community - Along with the growing popularity of the language, came to the growth of the community. There are many repositories, forums, blogs, and tutorials for you to learn how to program.

- Wages on the rise - The average salary for a Data Scientist who programs in Python is around $ 127,000 annually.

- Libraries - Libraries such as Pandas, Matplotlib, Scikit-learn, Seaborn, Numpy, Keras, Scipy, PySpark, and many others have become industry standard. No matter what your problem, there is probably already a library ready to import and use.

To give you an idea of the beauty of simplicity, see the same code written in Java and Python, where the goal is to open a text file.

Another aspect that gives Python a tremendous advantage is that it is generic. I can create an API, a backend for my application, build an interactive dashboard, or even create a face recognition system and put it on my Raspberry Pi!

Also, being interpreted allows you to be able to prototype your ideas quickly, speeding up the development cycle of any project.

The Dataquest site has identified that Python is the most widely used Python language for Data Science and that it should maintain a growing demand for the number of available positions, as shown in the image above.

The market has already assimilated and recognized the advantages of Python. This is even truer when it comes to Data Science.

Increasingly, vacancies are coming with this requirement of programming in language. For this reason, it is worth investing time to learn it.

www.ingramcontent.com/pod-product-compliance
Lightning Source LLC
Chambersburg PA
CBHW071115050326
40690CB00008B/1224